Here for a purpose

The inspiring story of
the artist Tom Yendell

Marc Alexander

Published by	Mouth and Foot Painting Artists
ISBN	978-0-9565384-1-3
Paintings	© Association of Mouth and Foot Painting Artists
Text	© Marc Alexander
Cover photo by	Ray Massey
Designed by	Foster de Kretser Graphic Design
	www.fdk.co.uk
Printed by	Arrowhead Printing Ltd
	Unit 1, Alton Business Centre, Omega Park,
	Alton, Hampshire GU34 2YU

At Tom Yendell's request, this book is dedicated to his friends Alyn and Leigh for their inspiration.

The author Marc Alexander with Tom during a visit to the
TEABAG project in Ghana.

Photo: Ray Massey

Foreword by Alan Titchmarsh

I can remember quite vividly when the thalidomide scandal broke in the late 1950s. It came in a year that brought other tragedies – I failed my 11 plus examination and was sent to secondary school.

But it quickly became apparent that my own misfortune was minor compared with those of the children who had been born that year with deformed or absent limbs, simply because their mothers had trusted and taken a drug that was meant to relieve morning sickness. Of the 2,000 babies who were born in Britain, only 466 survived. This is the biography of one of them, and it is quite an astonishing story.

Tom Yendell is a one-off. He is creative, determined and public-spirited, and he has a wicked sense of humour. He has needed it.

I remember once asking the late pianist Sir George Shearing if he had always been blind. 'So far', was his answer. I suppose you might put Tom in the same category, though as far as his arms go there is no hope of them ever returning. The lack of them has, astonishingly, not held him back one jot.

What Tom has done is to build on what nature gave him rather than complain about what man took away.

As a child he found that false arms simply impeded his activity, and at the age of 14 he vowed that he would never wear them again. Their absence has not held him back, neither has his creative ability been compromised. He is an accomplished artist with the Mouth and

Foot Painting Artists and added to this, his work with TEABAG in Ghana is a testament to his outward-looking rather than introspective nature.

When you read the story of his birth and his instant ability to use his feet where others use their hands I defy you not to be moved. What also impresses is Tom's total lack of self-pity. The title of this book reflects his attitude.

Tom and his wife Lucy are an inspiration to the rest of us, and the story you are about to read will engender in you a range of emotions – from anger and frustration to astonishment and amusement. Above all, it will enrich your life, which is something Tom seems to do quite unconsciously with everyone he meets.

Alan Titchmarsh

Preface

Tom Yendell was born on the morning of March 21st 1962 at Winchester Hospital, but before his mother Margaret had even seen her newborn son, the nurses had whisked him away.

'Where are you taking him?' she asked.

'You won't get him back,' was the callous reply.

Margaret was distraught and in the days that followed, still not having seen her baby, she would anxiously ask about him.

The usual reply was, 'Oh, we've just seen him. He's a lovely bouncing baby. So beautiful!' but still she wasn't allowed to see him and after a short while Tom was transferred to the renowned Stoke Mandeville Hospital in Aylesbury.

> Before his mother Margaret had even seen her newborn son, the nurses had whisked him away.

'I didn't see Tommy until he was about six weeks old,' Margaret says. 'I could sense that all was not well with him, but all the doctors would say was that my son's arms had not developed as well as they should have.'

Then, by the merest chance, Margaret saw a programme on television about the devastating effects of a drug prescribed to alleviate morning sickness, a drug Margaret herself had been prescribed, and at once she knew what had happened.

'I was shattered, I felt frozen. Tommy was a thalidomide baby.'

Tom's father Jack Yendell in Royal Marines uniform

Chapter 1

'The Child is father of the Man' wrote William Wordsworth in his poem "My Heart Leaps Up". It became one of his most quotable lines, expressing in seven words what was to become one of the main tenets of modern psychology. But if the personality of 'The Man' owes much to the character of 'The Child', the biographer should consider what shaped the 'The Child's' personality. Thus Tom Yendell's story begins long before he came into the world.

His father, Jack Yendell, a Somerset man with a farming background, was born in West Buckley in 1922. At the age of ten he was about to take his Scholarship Examination when he suddenly collapsed – not through fear of the exam but with acute appendicitis. Indeed it was so acute that he was hospitalised for several months and his hopes of a scholarship faded.

Four years later he left school and began work as an apprentice in a bakery. Hopeful of continuing his education and gaining qualifications that would enable him to get a better job, he spent his free time studying with a correspondence course. This continued until he realised how happy he was with the work he was already doing, and he resolved to become a master baker.

After the outbreak of war in 1939 Jack decided to join up and the thought of visiting faraway places urged him to choose the navy. While waiting his turn at the recruiting office, he fell into conversation with a sergeant in the Royal Marines. He explained to the sergeant that because of his ability as a baker, he had hopes of becoming a navy cook in order to gain experience in his trade.

'Listen lad,' said the sergeant. 'The marines have cooks as well as the navy and they get sixpence a day more than sailors.'

He was so enthusiastic about the service that Jack changed his mind about becoming a sailor in favour of joining the marines. To this day he declares it was the best decision he ever made.

Soon afterwards he was ordered to report at the Chatham naval base where his military career began with catering classes on *HMS Pembroke*. He also had to take more martial courses, gaining a high rating in gunnery, which resulted in him being transferred to *HMS Royal Sovereign*.

> The wedding proved that their 'love at first sight' had become an abiding bond that remains to this day.

During a few days' leave he returned to Somerset and visited some old friends on a farm. There he met a young nurse named Margaret who had come down from North Staffordshire to enjoy a holiday on the farm that her Aunt Lucy had continued to run after she was widowed.

Margaret, who had been born in the same year as Jack, had left school at 14, which was not unusual in those days. It was her ambition to become a nurse but she could not commence her training until she was 16. As a consequence, she found an interim job with a printing firm in Leek, working in the silkscreen printing department. When she reached the required age she started as a probationary nurse in the Leek hospital and at 18 commenced general training at Manchester.

On the pleasant Sunday that Jack arrived at the farm, Margaret had expressed a wish to go walking on the nearby Blackdown Hills. She had asked her cousin Fred to take her but he was too occupied with essential farm work.

'Jack might go with you,' suggested Aunt Lucy. Jack was happy to oblige and so they set off. A brief escape from wartime pressures, it turned out to be an idyllic walk. While cynics may regard the idea of 'love at first sight' as something that only occurs in a certain type of romantic novel, it certainly happened with Jack and Margaret.

They were only able to meet twice again before Jack sailed away on *Royal Sovereign*. From then on, their romance was conducted by frequent letters and though it was very rarely they were able to see each other during the next four years, they remained certain of their feelings for each other.

Royal Sovereign escorted convoys between such faraway places as Rangoon, Bombay and Aden, and in company with the Indian fleet patrolled the Indian Ocean.

In 1943 the ship's bows were damaged by enemy action. She sailed to America for repairs and remained in Philadelphia for a

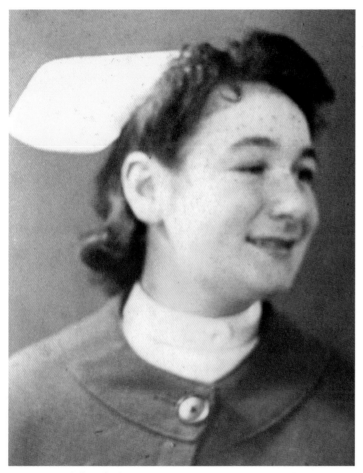

Margaret Yendell worked as a ward sister until the birth of her first child

year. During that period a *Royal Sovereign* football team was formed to play local teams, soccer being surprisingly popular in the city, no doubt because a large section of its population had emigrated from Europe.

Jack was an enthusiastic player until he received a severe knee injury during a match between the *Royal Sovereign* side and a local gasworks team. It was an injury that necessitated an operation, and still troubles him to this day. The gas workers expressed their regret over the accident by raising a fund for him.

After returning to England, *Royal Sovereign* was leased to the Russians, which meant that instead of rushing to Manchester to see Margaret, Jack had to spend a month aboard the ship training Russian gun crews. When at last he was able to meet her they both found that their mutual attraction was as strong as ever. Margaret still likes to talk about the dress – along with lipstick and stockings – that Jack had bought for her in America, where such valued items were still available.

Jack was next posted to *HMS Anson,* which sailed to the Pacific. On the voyage the marines learned that they were to take part in what they feared would be a suicidal landing on the Japanese mainland at Kobe.

'Thank God for the atomic bomb,' Jack declared to the author. 'If it were not for that I probably wouldn't be here today. We would not have stood much of a chance against the Japanese army on their own territory. It could have been a second Gallipoli.'

On August 6 1945, when *HMS Anson* and other invasion vessels were at sea, the atomic bomb was dropped on Hiroshima. Following a second bomb on Nagasaki, the Pacific war was over.

In 1947 Jack and Margaret married at Cheddleton in Staffordshire. They had spent no more than a total of four weeks together since they first walked on the Blackdown Hills. Nevertheless, the wedding proved that their 'love at first sight' had become an abiding bond that remains to this day.

The couple began married life in Plymouth, Jack still being in the Royal Marines where he worked in catering. He was then promoted to take charge of the kitchens and the Officers' Mess at Bickleigh outside Plymouth where his cooking was greatly appreciated. Prince Philip and King Hussein of Jordan were among the VIP guests he served.

Margaret worked as a hospital ward sister until their first child

Jack and Margaret on their wedding day in 1947

David was born in 1949. Amanda arrived two years later and was duly followed by Adrienne and Alice.

In 1953 Jack left the marines and for a year worked for an insurance company. He decided, however, that he would be happier at his old trade and in due course he became the manager of a bakery in Basingstoke. When the owner wished to expand, he acquired a business in Andover consisting of a restaurant, coffee bar and bakery, and offered Jack the position of manager. Jack happily agreed and the family moved once more.

The venture went well, but with his strongly developed sense of independence, Jack dreamed of having his own business.

One day when reading *The Master Baker* he came across a 'for sale' advertisement for a bakery in Leighton Buzzard. As it included accommodation suitable for a large family, it seemed to be exactly what he was looking for and so he bought it.

Arrangements were made for the takeover in due course, but it was the beginning of a stressful time for Jack. As well as preparing to move to Leighton Buzzard and assume his own business, Jack also felt honour-bound to continue with his job in Andover until a replacement was found. On top of all this, he was having to look after his four children, because Margaret had suffered a mental breakdown and had been admitted to a psychiatric hospital.

She was pregnant with her fifth child at the time and as a sedative for her depressed condition, as well as a remedy for her morning sickness, she was prescribed a new drug called thalidomide.

Later described as 'one of the biggest tragedies of modern times', thalidomide had been developed by the German pharmaceutical company Chemie Grünenthal, which had patented it in 1954. It was launched in Britain in April 1958 by the Distillers Company under the name of Distaval.

It was claimed to be highly effective as a tranquilliser, a painkiller and a treatment for insomnia. Most importantly, it was hailed as a cure for morning sickness and so prescribed to thousands of pregnant women to alleviate the unpleasant symptoms. Acclaimed as a 'wonder drug', it was prescribed in many countries.

But doubts were raised in the early 1960s when it was estimated that worldwide, more than 10,000 children had been born with missing limbs and other physical abnormalities, including defective internal organs. An Australian obstetrician named William McBride and a German paediatrician Dr Widukind Lenz were foremost in suspecting that thalidomide was responsible for the alarming number of unnatural births.

In 1961 Dr Lenz proved conclusively that the drug was harmful, though the Distillers Company still claimed that Distaval could be given to pregnant women in complete safety. However, it was withdrawn in Britain in the same year.

The Sunday Times led a vigorous campaign on behalf of the UK thalidomide victims and their families, but it was not until 1968 that the Distillers Company agreed to a compensation settlement to be distributed by the Thalidomide Trust.

Just before the settlement was reached, an editorial in *The Sunday Times* stated, 'In the decade since thalidomide was invented, marketed and withdrawn, it has become the symbol of the havoc that a technically complex society can wreak upon its own members. In almost every country where the miraculous new "tranquilliser" was sold, it caused a national disaster. In British terms, it was one of the worst of all peacetime accidents.'

On top of all the other pressures he was facing and his anxiety over Margaret's mental condition, Jack Yendell then had the shock of learning that the baby they had all looked forward to was one of the victims of thalidomide. Like other parents in similar circumstances, he wondered what sort of a future there could be for someone so cruelly handicapped.

Red Rose Day Chromacolour

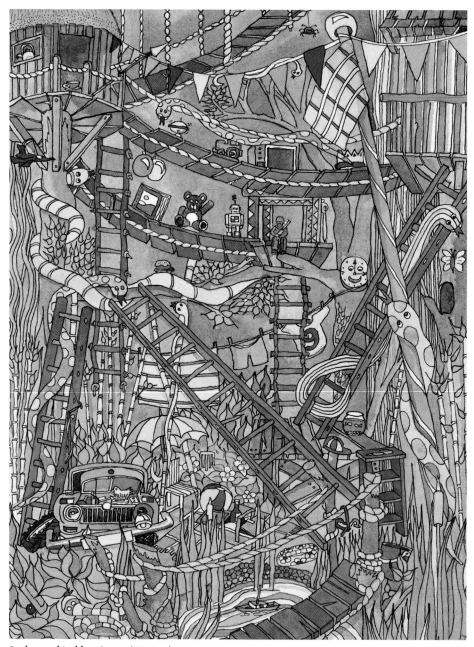

Snakes and Ladders Pen and Watercolour

City Hall Pen and Watercolour

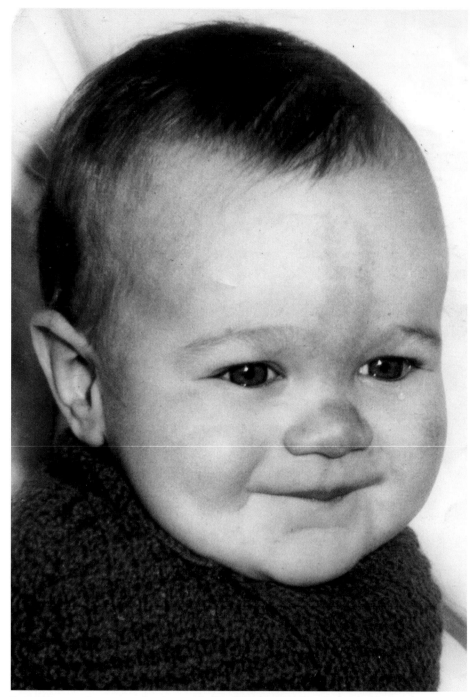

Tom at the age of one year, when he was finally allowed to leave hospital and go home

Chapter 2

No doubt baby Tom was transferred to Stoke Mandeville Hospital so that the doctors could study the effects of the 'wonder drug' that had taken the medical world by surprise. He was still there nine months after his birth, when on Christmas morning 1962, Student Nurse Bernadette Kerley walked into Ward 14. This was the first Christmas she would be away from her family in Ireland, and how she missed them. When she entered the ward the traditional tree with its baubles and twinkling lights just made her feel all the more lonely.

'Go and look after little Tommy,' the ward sister told her and she dutifully went to the cot where the nine-month-old baby lay gazing at the bright decorations. At the foot of the cot were several of the little presents that had been distributed to the young patients.

She picked up a striped woollen ball and held it for Tommy to see. He chuckled with delight and, using his feet, began playing with it. Bernadette's depression lifted at the sight of the baby having such fun despite his disability. His happiness was so infectious that her Christmas became one of love and goodwill.

'He was a wonderful, healthy little baby and so happy and pleasant,' she told the author. 'I think all the nurses fell in love with him. His disability did not seem to hinder him, indeed he could feed himself. He did this by lying on his back and holding the feeding bottle in position with his feet. Everyone thought he was a great baby.'

Time passed. Tom was finally discharged and Bernadette continued with her career, but over the years she wondered how life was treating Tommy whom she had come to regard as her 'special baby'.

She found out recently when she saw some Christmas cards produced by the Mouth and Foot Painting Artists (MFPA), and there was one signed 'Tom Yendell'. So strong were her memories of him lying in his cot that she wrote to him care of the publisher and in return has been gladdened to learn of his progress over the last half century.

Meanwhile, Margaret had returned home and understandably she feared it would be difficult to bond with Tom. When her other children had been born and she was caring for them at home, she had felt joy in motherhood. If only it could be the same with Tom, but nurses looked after his daily needs and she was a stranger to him.

'So he'll be all right. He won't play cricket for England but he will play football for Spurs.'

Talking about that anxious time Margaret says, 'When I was eventually allowed to visit Tommy at Stoke Mandeville Hospital where he was being treated, I remembered the publicity about other thalidomide children. I felt sick with worry before I went to the hospital for the first time, but I needn't have worried. I found a dear little cuddly baby wrapped up in his blanket.'

Once a week Margaret made the long journey from Leighton Buzzard to Stoke Mandeville where she could be with Tom, and then came a moment of great significance that still brings a glow of happiness to Margaret's face when she recalls it. As she bent over Tom's crib to change his nappy, the end of the scarf she was wearing fluttered down. A normal baby's reaction would be to recognise his mother and tug her scarf with tiny fingers. Smiling up at her, Tom did this with his toes. This symbolic gesture filled Margaret with happiness as at that magic moment she just knew that all would be well between them, regardless of the drug that was influencing their lives.

The excitement that the Yendell children had felt when they were told that they had a new baby brother soon turned to disappointment when they were unable to see him. All they wanted was for him to come home soon and so Jack and Margaret explained that he was not well. Then to prepare them for when he would come home, they explained that Tom was a dear little baby but he had no arms. This intrigued them and made them even more eager to see him.

Tom's sister Mandy recalls how she and her brother David had been to the Saturday morning cinema where they saw a newsreel about a severely paralysed American woman who had managed to bring up seven children. When Tom's disability was explained, David described the film vividly to the others and declared, 'So he'll be all right. He won't play cricket for England but he will play football for Spurs.' And after these reassuring words he went off to play football himself.

After some time the doctors agreed to let Margaret take Tom home for a trial weekend visit. His sisters and brother were delighted to see him, being fascinated by him rather than his disability, which, according to Margaret, they accepted 'with compassion and sympathy.' There were more home visits and finally it was decided that Tom could go home permanently.

Tom and his sisters celebrating his second birthday

Chapter 3

Thalidomide was still a matter of universal concern and Margaret was asked to provide a piece about Tom for a newspaper. She wrote: 'It was almost a year before my husband and I collected Tommy. What an amiable child he was, so good tempered. They were absolutely wonderful with him at Stoke Mandeville and I am sure he owes his happy disposition to their loving care.

'He fitted into our life as easily as each of the other children had done. At first we all wanted to do everything for him. It was instinctive, but I stopped it.'

Indeed Margaret went to great pains to prevent his sisters and brother from helping him. Both she and Jack believed that he should be left to his own devices in order to learn to do things for himself as much as possible. To ignore him when he was struggling was heartbreaking for the family yet they were encouraged by the way he developed the use of his toes just as an able-bodied baby learns to use his fingers.

Tom says that using his feet as his hands came to him quite naturally. He never needed to be shown how to manipulate them and always found ways of managing such things as drawing with a pencil held between his toes. Tom's sisters and brother accepted the fact that he was physically different from them and let him take part in robust family life as naturally as if he had no physical handicap.

'Our parents did not mollycoddle him and he was brought up

believing he could do anything,' David says today. 'For example, when he was born the experts said he could never walk yet by the time he was 12 months he was beginning to. He would sit with his bottom on the floor and endeavour to move about by pushing with his legs. The problem was that having no arms he was unable to stand up by holding on to the furniture or save himself when he was upright and lost his balance.'

However, David admits that he was disappointed when Tom was born, saying, 'I had three sisters and I really wanted a brother who I could have fun with. I realised that as he grew older we would not be able to play games.'

When Tom was taking his first unsteady steps, visitors would sometimes be puzzled by the sound of mysterious bumps.

'That's just Tom falling over,' the young Yendells would explain casually.

In order to avoid head injury Tom was provided with a special child-sized crash helmet. And so that he could practice walking safely, a baby walker mounted on wheels was found for him. As he could not grasp the handles, he managed by pressing his body against them, which allowed him to race about the house with great abandon.

Throughout his life Tom's motto has been 'Try everything' and this attitude goes back to his earliest days.

No doubt that while Tom understood that in some ways he was physically different from his brother and sisters, it did not seem to bother him. He taught himself to walk and run, pick up things with his toes and play with his toys.

One thing he found that he could not do was open a door. No matter how badly they wanted to turn the handle for him, the family made no move to help him. Standing alone for a long time by the door, he was determined to find a way. Throughout his life Tom's motto has been 'Try everything' and this attitude goes back to his earliest days. He finally solved the door problem by using his teeth to grip the handle and then move his head.

To stand back and let Tom struggle was distressing for the family. No doubt at times they had feelings of guilt even though they believed it was necessary for him to attempt everything possible by himself.

Today Tom says, 'I am very lucky that I had parents strong enough to treat me no differently from the others so that I had to learn to do everything by myself.'

Tom, his parents and siblings all dressed up for a family wedding

The Junkyard Pen and Watercolour

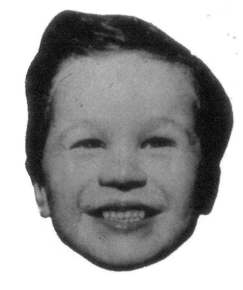

This child might have been **YOURS**

SURELY THIS MUST MAKE YOU THINK

Tom's photograph was used to raise awareness about children affected by thalidomide, as shown here on the cover of a leaflet published to raise funds.

Chapter 4

Following the Yendells' move to Leighton Buzzard, Jack was eager to make a success of the bakery he had bought. Apart from his enthusiasm for his chosen career, he was determined to do his best for his young family, especially the latest addition. He and Margaret wondered what the future would hold for Tom as he grew up. What opportunities could there be for someone who had been born without arms? How would he support himself in the years ahead? Jack wanted to be able to help him and provide some security if he was unable to be self-sufficient. And so Jack worked as he had never worked before.

Reminiscing on that time Tom's brother says, 'In those days, my father baked in the traditional way. The dough was allowed to sit for three hours before it was put in the oven to rise, and it would be moulded and put into a prover.

'At one stage he baked 20 different types of bread – French and Viennese bread, brown, wholemeal, rolls and things like that. It was a real old-fashioned bakery. Actually he was both a baker and a chef. Before we left Basingstoke he ran a café as well as a bakery with a lot of outside catering.

'He was an absolute champion at icing cakes, especially wedding cakes, and he became acclaimed for the way he decorated them. In those days it was the custom for the icing on wedding cakes to be virginal white but he began experimenting with colour. Blue and white icing, based on Wedgwood pottery, set a trend that gained him a reputation as an artist.

'He started in the bakery at 3 o'clock in the morning, had a rest at lunchtime and then worked until 6 o'clock. On Fridays he began baking for his weekend customers at five in the afternoon and worked until 9 o'clock on Saturday morning. On Sunday he only did eight hours. My mother was involved in the business, serving in the bakery shop.

'This meant that although they were very caring parents they did not have a lot of time to pamper Tom. He had to take the rough and tumble with the other kids and he grew up believing he could do anything.'

Tom soon demonstrated this trait to the surprise and gratification of his parents. He had been most intrigued when he saw his sisters sketching with their crayons and coloured pencils, and before long he strove to hold a pencil between his toes. Then, with a sheet of paper in front of him on the floor, he tried to imitate them. At first his efforts were colourful squiggles but he became more ambitious as he gained increasing control of his pencil.

The Beano comic was a great favourite with the Yendell children and Tom amused himself by copying its cartoon characters.

Talking about that stage in his life he says, 'My mother always reminds me that I enjoyed drawing houses, plans of imaginary buildings and designing rooms.' It was a portent of Tom's future interests.

It seemed quite natural to him to use his feet as other children used their hands. Later as an artist he painted not only by gripping a brush with his toes, but also by holding the handle between his teeth. Both methods are equally effective.

If some of the patrons who flocked to the shop presided over by Margaret had been able to see into the actual bakery, they might have been surprised to glimpse a flour-streaked child seated on a table holding the handles of a rolling pin with his feet, happily rolling lumps of dough into smooth layers that would be cut into amusing shapes.

Tom loved the bakery and once told the author, 'I think that if I had been born with arms, I would have become a baker like my father.'

Apart from rolling dough, there were other attractions at the bakery. One day Jack looked up and saw his disabled son standing alone on the bakery roof.

'We used to have a trolley with a framework on it for piles of baking trays,' Jack explains. 'Somehow he managed to climb up this to a wall and then get on to the roof. So I had to follow him up there. And later he was very good at tunnelling. He and his friend Graham dug an underground cave in the garden – it was a wonder they didn't get buried.'

Although Tom's parents were encouraged by the way he strove to be independent, they also had uneasy moments.

One of these occurred when his sisters took him to a park that had a high slide. Their problem was to get Tom up the tall ladder to the platform at the top and they decided to make him to do it by himself. The method was for him to mount the ladder by hooking his chin on each rung to keep his balance as he ascended. He loved it, climbing up again and again to hurtle down the slide. Margaret was aghast when the girls proudly described his achievement.

Tom on the slide at Leighton Buzzard recreation ground

****

One afternoon Jack and Margaret heard from the Thalidomide Trust that the American television company

CBS wanted to make 'a day in the life' film about Tom the next morning. They agreed to the proposal and shooting duly began at their home, commencing with Margaret strapping on Tom's artificial arms and sending him off to school. Then in the classroom he demonstrated how he used a pencil with his foot and recited "Two Little Dickie Birds" though without the traditional hand movements. The filming continued back at his home, concluding with Tom in his bath.

The story appeared in a local newspaper, which commented that he was cheerful and mischievous and 'not at all camera shy'.

One of Tom's most exciting moments came when he was given a tricycle, which he rode round the house at high speed.

Tom with his mother outside the bakery at Leighton Buzzard

'He used to guide it with his knees,' Margaret recalls. 'It had a box attached to it in which he carried his little gardening tools. He was a keen gardener and had his own little plot. It made me feel sad when I first saw him sitting down using his fork with his foot. Then I realised how happy he was. Sometimes I think he rather scorned the others because they could not use their toes like he did.'

Later his parents had a specially designed bicycle made for him by the Raleigh Cycle Company in Nottingham. In fact it was a forerunner of the chopper cycles that became so popular later on. Thanks to enthusiastic instruction from David and his sisters he soon learned to ride it.

Tom still enjoys cycling. His full-size bicycle was specially designed for him by engineers connected with Remap, a charitable society that specialises in devising aids for the handicapped. For mouth painters who do not have the mobility to reach all over their canvases, Remap also developed an adjustable easel powered by electric motors. By a simple control the artist can position it so the spot being painted stays within the range of his or her brush.

Jack and Margaret were further reassured when they met Dr Wilkie who was over from the United States to stay for a short while at Oxford. Like Tom he had been born without arms yet had a highly successful

Tom still uses a specially adapted tricycle to get around

career and was particularly interested in thalidomide cases.

'He visited us and showed me how he did everyday things,' Tom says. 'He was very successful, drove a car and had a family. This gave my parents a boost as they saw that, like him, it was possible their son could lead a normal life.'

****

It was a pleasant day in the park and the elderly lady sitting on a bench smiled indulgently at the little boy skipping towards her along a path. He was so active, twirling round at intervals and waving his arms like a dervish. Then – horror! The child's left arm suddenly shot out of his sleeve, flew through the air in an arc and landed at her feet.

Today Tom still chuckles when he recalls her expression before she realised that it was not a real limb but a prosthetic appendage that had come loose as he whirled it round. He had just been fitted with his latest pair of artificial arms and, on his way to show them off to his friends, discovered that by moving his body in a sort of hoola-hoop motion he could make his arms swing out and circle in imitation of a helicopter's rotor. He decided that playing helicopters was great fun.

To keep his feet warm in winter his grandmother knitted him special open-ended socks so that his toes remained unimpeded.

As there was obviously no cure for those born without limbs, medical minds concentrated on designing mechanical substitutes for thalidomiders – as they tended to call themselves. These 'robotic' arms, held in place by a body harness, would be capable of basic mechanical movements. Powered by compressed gas contained in cylinders, the patient might be able to control them by flexing his or her shoulder or neck.

'One of my very first memories of life at Leighton Buzzard goes back to when my artificial arms were to be fitted,' Tom recalls. 'They used plaster of Paris bandages to cover my whole torso to get my dimensions. A strip of aluminium was put down my back so that when the plaster dried, shears could be used to cut it open. I always remember how hot that plaster was and also the smell.'

From these casts the 'arms' were tailor-made to fit Tom's small body at the Nuffield Centre in Oxford where specialists instructed children in their use.

'The gas cylinder was about the size of a pint milk bottle which I wore across my shoulders and it made me look like a cross between Metal Mickey and an American football player,' Tom says, his dislike of the device still discernible in his voice. 'I had a hook at the end of one arm and a "pat-a-cake" hand on the other with movable fingers.'

Tom on his tricycle, wearing the prosthetic arms that doubled as helicopter blades

What upset Tom was that he had to wear socks and shoes when his artificial arms were ready. The medical view was that he would not try to use his new 'arms' because he was capable of doing so much with his feet. For this reason, Tom had always gone barefooted at home, and to keep his feet warm in winter, his grandmother knitted him special open-ended socks so that his toes remained unimpeded.

Encouraged by his parents, Tom dutifully endeavoured to use his artificial arms and hands but he had little success. He tried drawing with a pencil held in his pat-a-cake hand only to produce disappointing squiggles. Margaret also had misgivings. The arms themselves, their mechanism and the gas bottle seemed so heavy to be strapped on to a four-year-old.

Nevertheless, she felt she had to go along with medical opinion. In September 1967 she wrote in a newspaper article: 'I take Tommy every four months to the Nuffield Centre in Oxford where they have a special

Having no arms doesn't stop Tom taking part in sports activities

unit for disabled children. I was very nervous the first time I took him. I dreaded the whole thing – I don't know why. I was pleasantly surprised. About 50 other mothers take their children to this centre, two at a time. It isn't like a hospital; it's more like a hotel inside.

'In fact we lived in a flat there for a fortnight, learning how to manipulate the artificial arms and teaching our babies to use them.

'At first my husband and I were obsessed with the thought of these children's sufferings. Thalidomide was always in our minds if not on our tongues. Gradually we saw Tommy thriving and happy and got things into perspective. We worry about him of course but I have learned to live with the anxiety. I say Tommy is no different but he is and makes more demands on us. I must always be patient to console him and to comfort him when he is upset. Who knows what goes through the mind of a five-year-old like Tommy.

'The harness he has to wear for his artificial arms tends to make him look round-shouldered. Like most of these babies he is inclined to a little chest weakness and I am afraid the weight may lead to constriction. Sometimes at night in bed, when I go over the events of the day as most mothers do, I wonder if I am too hard with Tommy. But I am so afraid he may be spoiled and so be weakened when he grows up.

'My instinct is to envelop him in my love, to isolate him from the rough and tumble of growing up. I have learned, however, not to give way to these emotions. It would not be good for Tommy. His welfare is all that counts. Each day brings its problems, some could be important. Tommy took a dislike to his artificial arms. He is so naturally adept at using his toes instead of fingers that the harness irks him.

'What should we do? My husband Jack and I have discussed it. If we forced Tommy to wear the harness he could lose confidence in us. In the hope that this was one of these phases through which children pass, we compromised. Now I insist that Tommy wears his arms at lunchtime and uses his 'hands'. I sympathise with him as the harness weighs four and a half pounds; a lot of weight to carry around...'

When one of Tom's sisters returned home from school one day, she was dismayed to see him in floods of tears, sitting on his mother's lap and she equally tearful. She explained that Tom was upset because he did not want to wear his arms any more but the doctors were adamant that he should continue with them. Feeling that it would be wrong – even cruel – to make him continue with something that was causing him such obvious distress, she decided that he could choose if and when he would wear them.

At that time Jack and Margaret planned to have a family holiday. They chose to go to Butlins as it had plenty of entertainment and activities for the children. With his new freedom to choose when he wore his arms, Tom decided to have an arms-free holiday. Once when Margaret went into the Butlins ballroom where some children were playing, she was amused to hear a boy ask Tom where his arms were.

'In a box under the bed at home,' Tom replied, which of course they were.

When it was finally agreed that gas-powered arms were not a success with Tom and some other armless children, the decision was taken to replace the functional with the cosmetic. The idea was to make the children as 'normal' looking as possible and so limbs were designed to be as realistic as possible. There were 'veins' on the wrists and plastic fingernails on the fingers. Although the wearer could not move the arms, hands and fingers, helpers could fix them into various natural-looking positions.

After Tom was duly fitted with a pair, his playful sisters would bend two of his fingers into the position that Winston Churchill used for his 'V for Victory' symbol, which has come to have a different connotation.

When he looks back on the days when he wore prosthetic limbs,

Tom is still incensed at the medical profession's enthusiasm for them. He considers that attempts to make thalidomiders look as though they were able-bodied were self-defeating, as they actually drew attention to the wearer.

To give a child cosmetic arms, no matter how realistic they may appear, could have the opposite effect when, at bedtime, the harness was undone and the removal of the arms emphasised the difference between the wearer and his or her able-bodied siblings and playmates.

When he reached the age of 14, Tom gave up his false arms.

'I found them more of a hindrance than a help,' he says. 'They made me look more unusual because while I had them on, I still used my feet to do what hands normally do.'

Scenes suitable for Christmas cards are an important element of the work produced by MFPA artists and this image is typical of the style Tom has developed

Three Wise Men Silk Painting

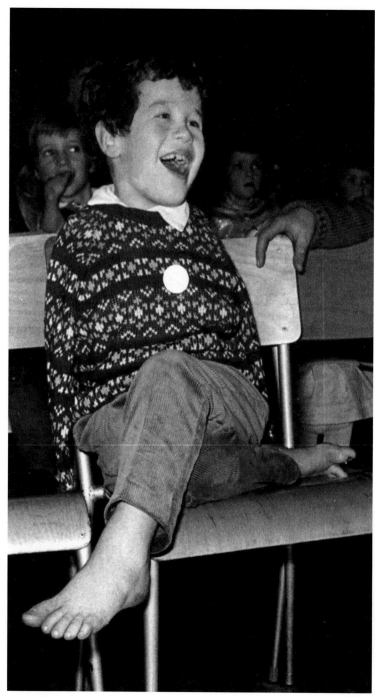

Tom enjoying an outing to a show

Chapter 5

And now a notable lady – in both senses of the word – enters the story. She was Lady Mary Hoare, the wife of Sir Frederick Hoare, Lord Mayor of London. Her interests extended beyond her obligations as Lady Mayoress and she was particularly concerned over the plight of disabled children. This was intensified with the advent of thalidomide, which was to affect more than 600 families in the United Kingdom.

With her well-known determination she initiated the Lady Hoare Trust for Physically Disabled Children, declaring 'These children are of normal intelligence. Their handicap is physical not mental, and it is our aim to help them lead as normal and active a life as possible.'

Another person who shared her view was a man named Peter Spencer. During the war he had enlisted in the RAF, gaining his 'Wings' in 1944. Assigned to Transport Command, he and his crew of three flew their Dakota – the renowned workhorse of the Air Force – on regular flights across the Channel, carrying supplies to the forward army units advancing through France following the D-Day landings.

When an urgent assignment came up on Peter's rest day he volunteered to fly four officers to Rheims in an Anson aircraft. As the station truck was taking the crew out to their plane on the tarmac a taxiing Mosquito bomber struck their vehicle with its starboard propeller. Peter's right arm was shorn off and his left arm was injured so badly he could never use it again.

After he was invalided out of the service, the Air Ministry department that dealt with the rehabilitation of injured airmen arranged for him to attend London's Central School of Speech Training and Dramatic Art in the hope he might get work with the BBC as an announcer. It was an imaginative idea. When it was considered he was ready he went for an audition. This was successful until it was realised that it would be impossible for him to turn the pages of a script or flick the necessary switches.

He returned to his parents' home in Wallasey and, making the most of his speech training, gave elocution lessons.

One day he read an item in a magazine about a disabled German artist named Erich Stegmann who painted with a mouth-held brush, and he decided to try the technique himself. He was so encouraged by his early attempts that he enrolled in the Wallasey School of Art. Later he joined the Mouth and Foot Painting Artists and became a professional artist.

A little boy crossed the floor in a series of somersaults despite the fact he had no arms.

In 1966 the members of the German MFPA organised an art exhibition in Frankfurt in which their paintings were sold for the benefit of thalidomide children. Peter Spencer thought that if such an event was successful in Germany, why not hold a similar one in England, and he put the idea to the Lady Hoare Trust. The suggestion of an exhibition of paintings donated by handicapped artists was welcomed because as well as fundraising, it would demonstrate that people with disabilities could still have useful and creative lives.

It was decided to hold the proposed exhibition at London's Royal Exchange. In order to publicise it, Lady Hoare held a reception at the Press Club to which not only journalists were invited, but also MFPA artists and parents of thalidomide children. Watching the arrival of the guests Peter Spencer was greatly amused when a little boy crossed the floor in a series of somersaults despite the fact he had no arms. Peter congratulated Jack and Margaret Yendell on their son's unrehearsed performance. From then on he kept in touch in order to follow Tom's progress and possibly influence it.

It was at the MFPA exhibition that Jack bought a picture by the disabled artist Richard Hext. His Dartmoor landscape fascinated Tom, especially when he knew it had been painted in the same way that he drew his pictures.

Richard Hext, whose painting was an inspiration to young Tom

Still Life in the Studio Silk Painting

Christmas Eve Silk Painting

Tom at Normans Bay

Chapter 6

Life in Leighton Buzzard continued to be busy and happy for Jack and Margaret. The bakery was flourishing and apart from baking Jack had great success with his cake decorating. As well as running the bakery shop, Margaret had five children to care for. It was decided that it would be best for Tom to attend a state school, as he would always be surrounded by the able-bodied in daily life. Accordingly he was enrolled in a nursery school, which he seemed to enjoy and later he went on to a church school.

From what Tom can remember of those days he says that he was not laughed at or teased on account of his disability. It seems the way he could do most things with his feet – coupled with a cheerful personality – earned his classmates' respect. However, there was one occasion when Tom was subject to bullying. One afternoon his brother came home to find him in tears with Margaret trying to comfort him.

'Jimmy hit me,' he told David between sobs. 'He laughed at me because I haven't got arms.'

'Listen,' said David. 'When you come home tomorrow I want you to bring me Jimmy's front teeth.'

Tom seemed so enlivened by the idea that Margaret was afraid that there would be mayhem in the playground, especially as Tom was strong for his years. She did not know exactly what happened the next day, but although Tom had not got Jimmy's teeth, he had been sent home for fighting. He had a very satisfied smile on his face and he never complained about being bullied again.

By 1971, the year of Jack and Margaret's 25th wedding anniversary, Jack had enjoyed running his bakery for several years. Then one day he was seized by an intense arthritic pain in his leg. It was so acute he could not remain standing and could hardly walk.

Ever since he had received an injury playing football in Philadelphia during the war, he was troubled by the old lesion. Now medical opinion was that there was no cure for the impairment, which had doubtless been aggravated by the exceptionally long hours he spent on his feet in the bakery. After a while he managed to walk short distances but there was no question of him continuing to work as he had in the past.

'Local people accepted us fairly quickly and soon got used to having a lot of funny-shaped young kids in the village.'

With the disappointment of having to give up the bakery and his highly satisfying occupation, coupled with the anxiety of providing for his family, Jack was facing a bleak future, but help was to come from an unexpected source.

****

Lady Hoare's concern for families that included a thalidomide child had made her well aware of the strain that they were under, so she decided to open a holiday home, where such families could relax and the children play away from the stares of the able-bodied. She owned a spacious house named Four Winds, which she believed would be suitable for her plan. It was ideally situated overlooking the sea midway between Eastbourne and Pevensey Bay, at a hamlet named Normans Bay, and as one would expect the name referred to William the Conqueror's arrival in that area in 1066. Later it became a base for smugglers who landed their contraband there, for distribution by small boats on rivers leading to the weald. This traffic ended in 1833 after a ferocious battle with the excise men.

Now the hamlet was happily peaceful, a perfect spot for what Lady Hoare had in mind. But such a project required rather special people to manage it and she knew just such a couple – Jack and Margaret Yendell. Jack had experience in catering and Margaret had been a professional nurse, they were certainly used to looking after children and they would understand the needs of disabled guests as they had experience in caring for their own incapacitated son.

For Jack the opportunity came just at the right moment. He and Margaret accepted the post and in 1971 a new chapter began when the Yendell family moved to Normans Bay. They were accommodated in an empty coastguard cottage next to Four Winds, where they spent most of their time. Jack took over the kitchen as resident chef. As there was no longer the need for the long periods of painful standing, which had been required at the bakery, it suited him very well.

Lady Hoare and her trustees wondered how the local residents would react to the presence of so many disabled children.

Looking back to those days Tom says, 'Normans Bay was a tiny little hamlet and the local people accepted us fairly quickly and soon got used to having a lot of funny-shaped young kids in the village. In fact they were very kind and made a concrete pathway over the sand so those confined to wheelchairs could be wheeled along the seashore. Every Friday the local newsagent gave away all his unsold comics to the visiting boys and girls. Another treat was when my father emerged from the kitchen to distribute freshly made doughnuts.

'While we were there we made a great number of friends, and we are still in contact with some of the people who stayed with us.

'Normans Bay was a little world of its own. For example, the railway line goes through the edge of the village and has a manual crossing gate even now. It was locked between 9 o'clock in the evening and 7 o'clock in the morning.

'Because the village was so out of the way, its road lacked the usual maintenance. It was up to the villagers to keep it in a fairly reasonable condition. Money to buy the tarmac for it was raised by an annual barbecue which developed into a village festival to which my father contributed his various cakes and so on.'

Four Winds suited Jack because he was still able to enjoy his chosen profession. Every Friday he would open the kitchen door and the locals would queue for his special fish and chips, the fish having come straight from the sea. This became another weekly treat for the children.

On Christmas Day, the Yendell family and the visitors would enjoy one of Jack's splendid meals in the spacious dining room at Four Winds. When it was nearly over, he would clutch his stomach and say as he left the room, 'I have a tummy ache and I must lie down.' Then, to the visiting children's amazement, Father Christmas complete with the traditional white beard, would suddenly appear with his sack.

✴✴✴✴

Tom found his new home to be idyllic. Where the cottage garden ended the shore began. Although there were shingle banks along the shoreline to Beachy Head, there was a stretch of sand ideal for castle building when the tide went out. It was great fun even if the castles had to be moulded by foot. As Margaret recalls, much of Tom's early drawing was sketching plans of imaginary buildings. Now he had the opportunity to fashion them out of damp sand, pebbles and tiny shells.

Soon after settling in at Four Winds, Tom was given a present that filled him with joy. It was a kitten so small that she could fit into a large matchbox. She was Tom's first animal companion and he named her

Sally, and Sally enjoyed being stroked by a foot just as much as if it been a hand. Today Smudge, Tom's lively spaniel, is equally happy to be foot patted.

When Tom was born it was found that he had a slight curvature of the spine. After the family moved to Normans Bay, medical advice was that horse riding might improve the condition, which it did. Tom joined the Riding for the Disabled Association and his equestrian lessons began. He found he enjoyed it immensely and as usual his feet made it possible. Two reins from the horse's bit were linked to the stirrups so he was able to control his mount in the same way that drummers in a cavalry band do, by foot movement. On one occasion he and a group of members went riding with Princess Anne, the patron of the association.

An aspect of Normans Bay that Tom greatly appreciated was the company of the children who came to stay at Four Winds. He could show them round and join in their own special games. Unlike schools where they were 'different' from the able-bodied pupils, disability was normal there and the games they invented reflected this.

To add to the enjoyment of the visiting children, Jack bought an inflatable dinghy. With the children safely strapped into their life jackets he would lift them into the boat and to their delight take them for a trip round the bay. For thalidomide youngsters it was a wonderful sensation to be riding the wavelets and it mattered not that some could not walk or use their arms – they were cruising just as though they were able-bodied.

When Robert, a little boy who had been born without limbs, was placed in the dinghy, he had a marvellous sensation of freedom, which he celebrated

Tom had his own way of keeping cool!

Tom learned to ride with Riding for the Disabled and was part of a group which met Princess Anne (opposite page), who was Patron of the Association

in an alarming manner. With a special life jacket encircling his torso, he somehow manoeuvred himself to the side of the boat and then rolled over into the water. He bobbed up and down with the waves, chortling until he was hauled back on board. To have found something so exciting that he could do all by himself was so important to him that Jack was always willing to take him out knowing that thanks to his special life jacket he was never in danger.

As Lady Hoare had intended, Four Winds was not only beneficial for the children but also for their hard-pressed parents. The effect of thalidomide had been so unexpected that there was little background experience to help families with its effects. Stress was inevitable for some of the parents who sought to do their best for their thalidomide babies. They had to accept that life had inevitably changed and suffer anxiety over what the future could hold for a severely disabled child.

Meeting other families with similar children was a welcome opportunity to discuss their mutual problems. Another benefit of Four Winds was freedom from curious stares that in ordinary circumstances greeted the children when they appeared in public places.

Tom's education was naturally a matter of concern to Jack and Margaret and it was decided to enrol him at the Pevensey and Westham School. This meant that each morning Tom and his sister Alice would hurry to the Normans Bay railway halt to catch a train for a brief ride to Pevensey and Westham.

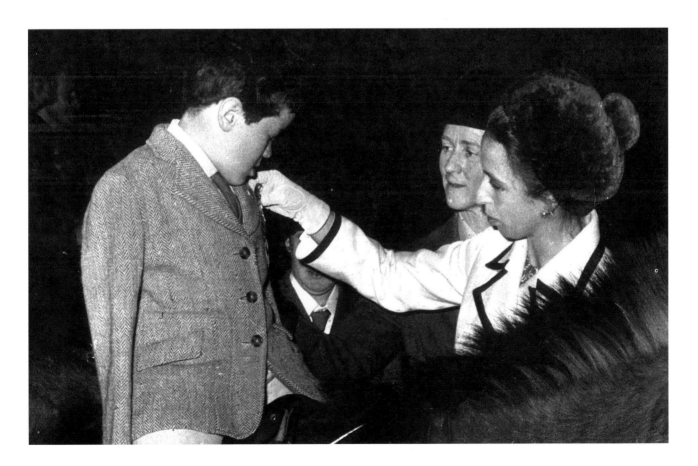

'The problem at the Pevensey school was that I was the only handicapped child there,' Tom says. 'The dinner ladies and the staff thought I was wonderful because of how I managed without arms. The teachers were quite happy for me to sit at the back of the classroom where I got away with doing as little work as possible.'

This suited Tom. He explains, 'I was lazy and all my way though primary school my parents, who did not think I was unintelligent, got frustrated by my lack of progress and the fact that I was not being pushed.'

It is easy to understand their anxiety over their son's future. In the nature of things it would be difficult for him to remain housebound later on. Apart from other considerations, they knew that his love of independence would not allow him to accept that. Yet what sort of work could someone without arms do? At least if he had a good education it would increase his chances of self-sufficiency.

'As I looked up, I saw her face with the sun shining behind her head like a halo.'

Because of his lack of progress, it was decided that he should go and board at a prep school named Temple Grove just outside Uckfield. There it was hoped he would be 'pushed' if necessary. For Tom it was a very big step to leave his family where he had been so secure. Recently he found a letter that his mother had sent him, written just after he left Normans Bay, praising him for being a 'brave boy' over the way he left home without fuss or tears.

It was arranged that he would stay with the school chaplain. Religion was an important part of the curriculum and Tom can still recite, in correct order, the names of all the books of the Bible. And it was at Temple Grove that hymns became one of his favourite forms of music, as they are still.

'The chaplain had three daughters,' he recalls with a reminiscent smile. 'Lydia was the oldest. She was a beautiful girl and all the boys were madly in love with her.'

To Tom, one of the best aspects of Temple Grove was that it possessed an outdoor swimming pool. He was already a good swimmer, having learned early with a pair of special water wings, which had been made at Stoke Mandeville. They consisted of polyester and wood with Velcro straps that fitted round his body.

'When I used to be taken to a swimming pool my brother David got so fed up with having to put these wings on me that one day he just pushed me into the pool and told me swim without them,' Tom says 'And so I swam.' Thus Tom felt quite confident when boys at Temple Grove had to qualify for their bronze, silver or gold swimming certificates.

'For one of them we had to do life saving,' he explains. 'This meant that you had to swim with clothes on, and so we were told to bring our pyjamas for the next swimming lesson.

'We lined up at the deep end, the teacher said, "Jump!" and we jumped in. All the other boys used their arms to keep their pyjama jackets down round their bodies but there was nothing I could do when my jacket came up and over the top of my head. The wet fabric clung to my face and I could not breathe.

'I was getting terribly worried about it so I kicked my legs as hard as I could and jammed my chin on the side of the pool where I struggled to get air through the soaking material. It had become a very frightening situation as there was no way I could remove my jacket. I felt I was suffocating.

'Then I heard a voice saying, "Are you all right, Tom?" It was Lydia and leaning over she undid the buttons of my pyjamas so that I could draw breath. As I looked up, I saw her face with the sun shining behind her head like a halo. It was absolutely gorgeous.

'That moment taught me that when I was going to do something that could possibly be difficult for me, I had to think twice about it.'

* * * *

As time passed, the number of visitors to Four Winds decreased. The 'thalidomide babies', all of a similar age, were growing into teenagers, and paddling and the building of sandcastles no longer held the same attraction. They wanted to be 'cool' and therefore holidays were taken further afield in popular resorts.

'Over the years fewer and fewer beneficiaries came,' says Tom. 'A new holiday home had been set up in Jersey and the Lady Hoare Trust found it increasingly difficult to keep Four Winds going. My parents would liked to have taken it over but for some legal reason it had to go to another charity. It was something that was set out in the deeds.

'So we moved to Bexhill on Sea. Here my parents bought a large house called Kennilworth, which they converted into a rest home for several elderly, non-smoking ladies. They were lovely and spoiled me, and when we chatted over meals, I found them to be very jolly and interesting.'

According to Tom, Lady Hoare could not have chosen a better place than Normans Bay for a holiday home. Today the seaside village retains its attraction, having a recreation site with pitches for tents, caravans and motorhomes. The spirit of relaxation and fun that the guests of Four Winds savoured, lingers on.

Poppies Watercolour Painted by Foot (All other paintings in this book were painted by mouth)

One of the many activities that Tom has tried over the years is shooting

Chapter 7

In June 1907 Sir William Purdie Treloar was pleased to write in his diary that Her Majesty Queen Alexandra '...came to the Mansion House to open the Queen's Fete in aid of my Cripples' Fund.'

Sir William, then Lord Mayor of the City of London, was concerned over the plight of city children suffering from respiratory ailments and tuberculosis. It was his conviction that above all, such children needed clean country air. To this end he launched a Cripples' Fund as a mayoral appeal, to finance a residential hospital and school in a healthy environment.

It was so successful that the following year the Lord Mayor Treloar Hospital and School for the Physically Disabled – generally known as 'Treloars' these days – was opened in Alton, Hampshire. It has retained traditional links with London in that every Lord Mayor of the City of London automatically becomes a trustee of the Treloar Trust and makes a yearly visit to the school accompanied by the Masters of many of the City livery companies.

Today Treloars is partly a specialist school for disabled children aged from 9 to 16, and partly a college for handicapped students aged 16 and over. In both cases the aim is not only to provide a sound education but also develop the pupils' abilities to enable them to become as independent as possible.

While Jack and Margaret were still at Normans Bay, they heard of how well children were catered for at Treloars and considered the possibility of Tom being enrolled there. They were worried because he had not made the progress they had hoped for at prep school.

Tom's sister Mandy describes how their mother had worked hard to coax Tom to read when he was younger. Margaret would sit beside her son trying to interest him in some book suitable for his age but he would not respond. He preferred to sit on the floor and draw.

'I was not academic,' Tom admits with a grin when he hears Mandy recounting that aspect of his young life. 'And I'm not academic now.'

According to Tom, the problem with a disabled child like himself going to a school for the able-bodied is that teachers are not accustomed to handicapped pupils, no matter how kindly they feel towards them.

He says, 'I used to be settled comfortably at the back of the class but I was not expected to do my lessons like the others. It suited me because it was a time in my life when I was happy to do as little as possible.'

'I was in tears. If I wore shoes how was I going to do anything?'

He believes that disabled children should go to appropriate schools, where staff experienced in specialised teaching are geared to bring out whatever abilities the children may have.

'Among the various careers that my mother thought might be suitable for me were tea tasting and working as a translator because they were two things you didn't need hands to do,' Tom says. 'My parents wanted me to have a go at everything it was possible for me to do. When I was small and we lived at Leighton Buzzard, we children used to go to the Saturday Venture Club and one of the things I did there was Irish Dancing, for which you do not need to use your arms. I really enjoyed it.'

When Tom's parents decided to send Tom to Treloars, Margaret took him to look around it.

'I remember my mother saying it was an awful place because she saw a boy having an illicit cigarette and heard another swearing and thought it would be bad for me,' Tom remembers. 'But it was one of the best things that ever happened to me. It made me independent, made me the man I am.'

However, his first day at Treloars was not a happy one. He was wearing special leather flip-flops, which he could easily slip off in order to use his feet and toes as the able-bodied use their hands. After his arrival he was summoned to the medical centre where the matron demanded, 'What are those things on your feet? Go back to your house and get some proper socks and shoes on.'

'I was in tears,' Tom recalls. 'If I wore shoes, how was I going to do anything?

'But times at Treloars were changing because up until then, the school had mainly enrolled haemophiliac and spina bifida pupils. With the arrival of thalidomide kids, the staff had to adapt to us but because they were already dealing with impaired children it became quite easy for them to do so.'

When Tom went to Treloars he wrote with his feet until he got too big to sit on a table in the classroom. In order to sit like his classmates he had to develop a new way of writing and drawing so he used his mouth to hold his pencil or brush.

Talking about his technique today, he says it has gone round in a circle as he has started using his feet again to paint as it is a lot freer.

No doubt against his will, Tom brought his 'cosmetic' arms to school, where he had no use for them except to have some fun.

He explains, 'The kid in the room next to me was called Kevin and Kevin had artificial legs. When there was a new member of the night staff we used to make a realistic dummy with our clothes and prosthetic limbs and put it under a bed with one of my arms sticking out. The night staff would come around and, startled to see the arm, pull out a body – to find it headless! It was the only use I had for my artificial arms.'

The seven years that Tom was at Treloars were happy and formative.

'People look back on who was the most important teacher in their life,' says Tom. 'For me it was my art teacher Alyn Wilde. He was an incredible artist and he really inspired us to try everything. We not only painted, we also did clay, we did wicker work.'

Alyn Wilde soon recognised Tom's artistic talent and did all he could to develop it. When Tom talks about him as a friend as well as his teacher, he says that he was the most important artistic influence in his life.

****

Tom went to live with his parents at their Bexhill guesthouse when his course at Treloars ended in 1980. The question of what he should do next did not present a problem. Thanks largely to Alyn Wilde's encouragement with his drawing and painting ability he decided to study art and began a foundation course at Hastings College of Art. The fact that he had to do his work with his feet was no hindrance and while his years at Treloars had been some of the happiest he had known, he thoroughly enjoyed his new surroundings.

When he had successfully completed his foundation year, Tom enrolled at Brighton Polytechnic to take a degree course in Expressive Art. This not only included painting and the history of art, but also drama and photography, subjects that he found very agreeable. Yet while he got on with his studies, at the back of his mind there was a vague sense of unfulfilment. In fact it was something that affects many people with disability; a basic need to have a sense of independence no matter how capable they are.

Those around Tom are often amazed by the way he can look after himself. At the dinner table he needs no one to help him. Seated in a suitable posture somewhat akin to the 'lotus position' with his knife and fork held firmly by his toes he can eat with the same ease as an able-bodied person.

Drinking from a glass or cup presents no problems either. He leans forward and takes hold of the rim of the glass firmly with his teeth and then tilts his head back to drink. People seeing this for the first time often fear that he is in danger of biting out a piece of glass. They need not worry, Tom is an expert at such routines.

But no matter how well disabled people are cared for, or how well they cope with their handicap, there is a subconscious yearning for the sensation of independence; to feel free from the restrictions that their condition imposes. To many, the symbol of personal freedom is the motor car. In their imagination the car is like a magic carpet that will whisk them to the corner shop, or carry them to Paris. And most importantly, sitting at the wheel gives the driver the elation of being completely in control.

It was not unusual that Tom, now 18, should be interested in cars like other young men, and added to this was the psychological independence factor. As a thalidomide beneficiary he received some compensation money, which enabled him to buy a silver Mini Clubman, which was to become one of the joys of his life.

The next step was to get the car adapted. An engineering company that specialised in such work fitted a large disk to the floor in front of the driver's seat. It was linked to the steering system and operated by the driver's right foot. The accelerator and brake were controlled by the left foot. Switches for lights, windscreen wipers and radio were positioned so that Tom was able to have exactly the same capability as an able-bodied driver.

He now had to learn how to drive. In his new car he had tuition with a driving school. After ten lessons he was ready to take the test.

One can imagine his elation when he was told that he had passed on his first attempt. Since then he has driven avidly, not only in England but also in other countries that he has visited.

'Being able to have mobility is one of the most important things that has happened to me,' Tom says. He adds with a grin, 'When I'm driving, the steering wheel still moves as I steer with my foot. This gives the illusion to pedestrians and other drivers that the car is steering by itself.'

Tom's other 'independence' objective was to have a place of his own, a place where he might prove to himself that he could be entirely self-sufficient. Thanks to compensation money he was in a position to start looking for a suitable abode.

It was around this time, in his second year at Brighton, that Tom joined a PHAB youth club, the letters being an acronym for Physically Handicapped and Able-Bodied. At that time Rolf Harris, a supporter of handicapped people, was president of the society, which had been established in 1957. The object of PHAB, in its own words, 'is to promote and encourage people of all abilities to come together on equal terms, to achieve complete inclusion within the wider community.' Today there are nearly 200 PHAB clubs throughout England and Wales.

'I steer with my foot. This gives the illusion to pedestrians and other drivers that the car is steering by itself.'

Tom not only enjoyed the social mingling of the disabled and the able-bodied at the club, but also became aware of a hitherto unrecognised aptitude when he became a youth club leader for the society. In doing this he not only found that he was a born organiser but also that he got tremendous satisfaction out of it.

As will be seen further in this book, Tom's enthusiasm for organising always has a beneficial motive. No doubt because he succeeded in surmounting his own inherent problems, he is glad when he can apply the same determination to the advantage of others.

****

After his first year at Brighton Polytechnic, Tom had a feeling of discontent. At Hastings College of Art he had found his lecturers to be very supportive but at Brighton he had a sense of being on his own. Added to this he felt he had seen little of the world outside school and college life. So he took a sabbatical year and was intent on making the most of it.

He became a youth club leader not only for PHAB but, with his newly-formed interest in such work, he also became involved in a new caring enterprise.

'One of the teachers at Treloars called Val Fephney started a charity called CRYPT – Creative Young People Together,' Tom explains. 'Val had three children who all had severe muscular disability. They were very creative and studied at Treloars but Val realised there was nothing for them when they left the college. Her idea was to set up houses round the country where handicapped children who were creative could live together and be helped and cared for by able-bodied young people who also had creative talents.

'So I did some fundraising for CRYPT which included organising a sponsored fun run across the marshes at Bexhill.'

It was during Tom's sabbatical year that he learned that Alyn Wilde, his art master at Treloars, had died unexpectedly. It was his first bereavement and he was devastated over the death of the teacher and friend who had given him so much encouragement. When he was invited to go to Treloars to take over Alyn Wilde's art classes until the end of the year, he willingly agreed.

Technicians at Brighton Polytechnic devised a frame that enabled Tom to use a camera

It was at this time that Tom thought about getting in contact with the Mouth and Foot Painting Artists. The disabled artist Peter Spencer had kept in touch with Jack and Margaret ever since he had seen little Tom turning somersaults at Lady Hoare's reception. He now suggested that as Tom enjoyed painting and drawing, he might possibly become a student of the unique co-operative someday.

Tom was intrigued by the idea but felt that his work had not reached the standard he wanted before submitting it. Perhaps when he had spent another year on his art studies he might try again.

After Tom's sabbatical ended, he returned to Brighton Polytechnic where photography, part of the Expressive Art course, became of particular interest to him.

It was no problem for Tom to operate his Canon camera with his feet but he was unable to manoeuvre it at the same time. Even with a tripod it was extremely difficult and his pictures were shot from very odd angles.

The technical staff at the college came up with the answer. A metal frame was designed that fitted on his shoulders with straps and two metal supports that rested against his chest. With the camera fitted firmly on the frame a few inches from his face, he could see into the viewfinder – no digital screens in those days – and line up his picture by positioning his body. Two model aircraft wheels were part of the mechanism fitted on the frame to control exposure and timing. Tom adjusted these and the shutter button with his chin.

One thing he was unable to do was develop his films, which was part of the course. It was one of the very few things that have eluded him but the darkroom work was done for him by a member of the technical staff.

Such was Tom's fascination with camera work that later he actually worked as a professional photographer.

Meanwhile he was about to experience one of the important episodes in his life. The ownership of a car had increased his self-confidence yet there remained one more requirement that he felt was necessary for a fully independent lifestyle – a place of his own. He house-hunted in Lewes, which would be conveniently close to Brighton.

His quest ended when he found a small terraced house opposite Lewes prison and bought it with compensation money that Jack had prudently invested for him.

Although it needed work, Tom thoroughly enjoyed preparing it for occupation. He purchased furniture, some of it comfortably inflatable, and kitchen utensils – Tom enjoys cooking – and began working out how he would tackle domestic jobs that to the able-bodied were routine chores. For example, how would he cope with washing-up? But he had no doubt that he would manage and soon proved that he could.

On an early visit Margaret found her son in such an enthusiastic and excitable mood over his new home that she was reminded of an ebullient character in *The Wind in the Willows* and promptly christened the house 'Toad Hall'.

✻✻✻✻

After Tom settled in Toad Hall he was invited to have Christmas dinner with his sister Alice. She asked him if he could buy a small turkey for the celebratory dinner so he duly set off to a supermarket.

'When I went over to a big freezer cabinet I saw there was a great big gap in the centre of the crushed ice where customers had taken out most of the frozen birds,' Tom recalls.

'There was a turkey at the bottom of the hole but obviously I could not lift it out so I decided to grip its wrapping with my teeth. I leaned forward to try and reach it but I slipped and fell head first into the hole. I was trapped. My shoes had fallen off, my shorts slipped down to my hips so only my bare legs appeared above the cabinet.'

A supermarket sales assistant could hardly believe her eyes at what she saw in the frozen food section. A pair of pale legs, rather male in appearance and kicking wildly, protruded from one of the refrigerated cabinets. She edged closer to the frantic limbs and heard Tom's voice yelling, 'Pull me out! Somebody pull me out!'

'I cannot touch a man's legs,' she cried indignantly. 'I shall have to call the manager.'

The disembodied legs continued to jerk energetically and a small crowd gathered to witness the bizarre display. The manager arrived, and with the help of a male assistant heaved on the legs until the rest of the shivering captive was freed from the ice.

When recounting the story Tom says it was the funniest incident in his life.

The Ship Pen and Watercolour

Abstract Watercolour

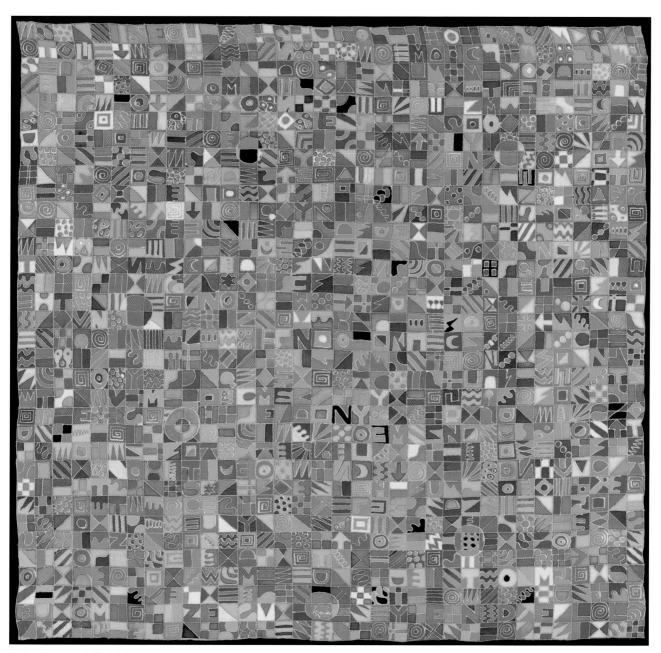

Design for a Scarf Silk Painting

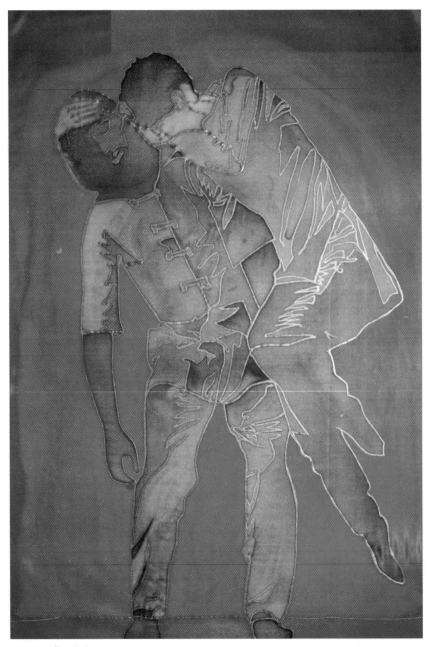

Dancers Silk Painting

Chapter 8

One evening Tom went to the PHAB club where a Mel Brooks comedy film *The History of the World* was to be shown. The laughter of the audience filled the hall but none laughed louder than Tom in the front row. It was just his sort of movie.

At the back of the hall a young woman named Lucy Nankivell was equally amused and laughed almost as loudly as a man at the front. When the film ended and the PHAB members mingled she recognised the owner of the loud laughter and soon they were chatting about the film they had just seen. Such are the workings of destiny.

Apart from their mutual admiration for Mel Brooks, Tom and Lucy found they had other interests in common. Although their paths had not crossed until then, Lucy was taking a foundation course at Brighton Polytechnic, prior to studying for a degree in art.

In recalling their first meeting, Lucy says that they both felt a mutual attraction.

'Definitely,' Tom agrees. In fact it seemed that their meeting had echoes of Jack and Margaret's first outing on the Blackdown Hills. And there were to be other similarities.

By the end of the evening Tom had invited Lucy to the house warming he was arranging for Toad Hall.

In describing her background Lucy says, 'I have two brothers, one older, one younger.

'My mother was a teacher and my father an electrical engineer and an enthusiast for Jowett cars. He has written books about them. I had a very happy childhood and I think growing up in the '70s was great fun.

'Everything was quite laid back and though we didn't have mobiles and all that sort of paraphernalia that children have to have today, we certainly had fun.'

And she and Tom certainly had fun as their relationship developed, although it was overshadowed by the fact that soon Lucy would be leaving to go to Bath University.

****

A third of Tom's Expressive Art course at Brighton Polytechnic was devoted to drama.

'For my theatrical degree I based my thesis piece on a man called Thomas Crippen who was a fairground attraction in Victorian times,' Tom recalls. 'He had no arms and he used to do things with his feet and his mouth to entertain the crowds.

'So when I had to do my theatrical performance we made a massive pair of dummy arms, each about 10ft wide. They did up at the front like a jacket. On the stage, I stood against the curtain at the back with these huge arms on.

'When the act started I had a friend of mine come on dressed as a ring master who announced, "I would like to introduce the world-famous..." and at his words, I jumped out of the arms and all I had on was a pair of Speedo swimming trunks. I did a couple of somersaults and then a variety of things with my feet. I think it was my way of "coming out". People who had been on the course with me who may have thought they knew what I'd look like under my clothes, could now see that I'm quite beautiful!'

Soon after this 'happening' Tom gained his BA with honours.

His university days ended, but Lucy's were about to begin at Bath for her three-year art course. It was a dismal thought because their relationship had been steadily deepening.

After Lucy started her studies, Tom would often drive his Mini to Bath to see her. One day they went shopping in a Sainsbury's supermarket. It was hardly a romantic setting but this did not deter Tom and he asked her to marry him. Her reply was that if he meant it, he would have to propose properly. He immediately dropped to his knees by a crate of tinned carrots and they became engaged, no doubt to the acclamation of nearby shoppers.

Again there was a similarity to Jack and Margaret's courtship that survived time and distance.

After completing his studies, Tom was faced with the prospect of finding work.

He realised that there were few jobs available for someone without hands, but with self-confidence built up over the years, he was convinced he would find employment sooner or later. In fact an opportunity came sooner than he expected.

The husband of Tom's sister Mandy had a brother who was in contact with a company named Business in the Community. It is one of The Prince's Charities, a group of not-for-profit organisations of which the Prince of Wales is President. Set up in 1982, its stated aim was to assist people starting up businesses. It has grown to be a 'business-led' charity that advises and challenges its members to 'create a sustainable future for people and the planet', and improve business performance. It now has a membership of over 800 companies, ranging from those with well-known

Tom and Lucy at Tom's graduation ceremony

brand names to small local enterprises.

Through the family contact, Tom went for an interview with the chief executive officer in London. At that point he had been doing a lot of photography, which was fortuitous as he had samples of his work to prove his ability with a camera. The manager explained they were looking for someone who would go round visiting people who had just started their own businesses, get their story and take photographs for the company newsletter.

Tom must have made a good impression because he was offered the job and happily accepted it.

When he took the train to London for his first day's work he must have wondered how a photographer without arms would be received but once he

Tom and Lucy became engaged after Tom had proposed on a shopping trip to Sainsbury's

had his camera fixed to his metal harness he was soon accepted as a professional.

'One of my first assignments was to photograph the work of two men who had just started a partnership after meeting in a pub and discussing art,' says Tom. 'One was a potter and the other an out-of-work tiler.

The potter explained that his wife wanted a ceramic tile picture on her bathroom wall but while he could paint and fire the tiles he could not set them in place.

'Of course that would be no problem to the tiler. Pooling their talents, they started a small company and won a contract with a well known chain of butchers to decorate the walls of their shops with tiles depicting arty cuts of meat. Their story inspired me with the idea of being my own boss.'

Meanwhile, Tom's interest in the MFPA increased when he visited an international exhibition of members' paintings at the Royal Festival Hall in London.

To Tom, the event, which was widely covered by the media at the time, was one of the most exciting he had experienced.

'It was an eye-opener to see the amazing pictures that had been painted by mouth or foot, and to meet the artists who inspired me to become involved,' he says.

＊＊＊＊

Tom had never been so busy. He was commuting to London every day to work full-time as a photographer, there were household chores at Toad Hall to be taken care of, and any free time he could find was spent at his easel. Best of all were the happy hours he was able to share with Lucy when he visited Bath. Yet apart from all this, he still somehow managed to maintain his interest in PHAB and local youth clubs. The idea of helping young disabled or disadvantaged people was becoming a strong feature of his personality. And there is no doubt that Tom was a born leader and relished every opportunity to get involved in fundraising and other such charitable events. No doubt his disability gave him empathy with those who had similar problems.

Because of such activities, coupled with the way he managed to cope with everyday life, people sometimes said to his mother, 'You must be proud of your son.'

'She never admitted it,' says Tom. 'I suppose she was so used to me that she'd merely reply, "Just what I expected." On one occasion I was interviewed on the Midweek programme by Libby Purves and Mum knew nothing about it. She was in the kitchen and when she switched on the radio she heard someone talking about how he managed without arms. She was interested because he was a thalidomider and, she said, listening to him made her feel really good. At the end of the programme there were the usual credits and when it came to "Thanks to Tom Yendell" she was so amazed, she nearly fell over.'

In the summer Tom and Lucy went to Greece for their first holiday together. Unfortunately it was during a great heatwave, which was so intense that there were numerous cases of people dying of heat stroke, especially in Athens.

'It was so hot, even at night, that we put wet flannels in the freezer and when they were frozen into wedges we would wipe ourselves with them to get some relief,' Tom remembers.

Although they experienced discomfort due to the freak weather, the important thing was that they were together.

> He began working his way round the kitchen with flame spurting from his foot to burn off the peeling paint.

Back in England Tom came to a difficult decision regarding Business in the Community. His daily commuting between Lewes and London, coupled with the extensive travelling his work required, was starting to adversely affect his health. Also, in the hope of becoming an artist with the MFPA, he wanted to concentrate on painting, so he resigned from the company.

His other weighty decision was to find a new house. Toad Hall had proved to Tom that it was possible for him to live completely on his own and he had thoroughly enjoyed his role as a householder. But now he felt he needed a larger place where there would be plenty of room for himself and Lucy when they married and, most importantly, where he could have a proper studio for his art work.

As he no longer had a regular job, the possibility of working on his own was uppermost in his mind. Inspired by the example of Peter Spencer who had achieved great success, Tom reasoned that with his aptitude for art, his most likely chance of achieving his ambition would be with his paintbrush.

Meanwhile, he found a house romantically named Hunter's Moon, which seemed just what he and Lucy were looking for. It was rather isolated, standing in a lane three miles from the main road between Seaford and Newhaven. It was in desperate need of renovation but it compensated with glorious views of the Sussex Downs.

What delighted Tom about the old place was that it had once belonged to an artist whose spacious studio stood at the bottom of the garden.

'The house needed a lot of work,' Tom recalls. 'I remember my mum in tears when she came to see it because it was in such a state. Uninhabitable really. Even so, I thought it was just beautiful.'

The old house may have looked beautiful to Tom but he did not have the same opinion of the interior. The refurbishment it required was daunting, but if it could be accomplished, Tom and Lucy were sure it would be rewarding. The Mini Clubman made frequent trips to DIY stores, to return loaded with building materials.

In her vacation Lucy joined Tom in the redecorating. They began work on the kitchen whose time-stained walls had deteriorated due to age, damp and a long period of neglect.

'The plaster had to be renewed and the ancient paint on the skirting boards was in a shocking state,' Lucy says. 'In those days Tom sometimes wore wooden clogs when he was working because they were easy to shake off if he needed to use his toes. So he screwed a blow-lamp to his left clog and strapped a wire brush to the other foot and began working his way round the kitchen, a flame spurting from his foot to burn off the peeling paint. Then he changed the blow-lamp for a scraper to clear away the charred debris and when that job was completed a paintbrush replaced the scraper.'

After Lucy returned to Bath, Tom lived alone at Hunter's Moon, working long hours on the house and painting in the garden studio in order to improve his skill as an artist. Having always had people around him, whether at home or at college, he was acutely conscious of the solitary life he was now living. A day could pass without him seeing a single person walk past his gate. When the famous Great Storm unexpectedly struck England in 1987, trees were blown down across his road so that he was completely isolated for three days.

Nevertheless, Tom still found time to do voluntary work with maladjusted children at the local school. He wanted to show them that if someone without arms could achieve a satisfactory life, it should be possible for them to do the same. Because of this attitude and personal experience of disability, Tom was asked to advise British Rail on how to improve their service for disabled people. He also helped St John Ambulance to organise holidays for handicapped children in the New Forest.

This charity work received recognition when he was chosen as one of the twelve 'Men of the Year' by RADAR, the Royal Association for Disability and Rehabilitation. Tom was invited to London's Savoy Hotel where he received his citation from Lord Tonypandy in company with such diverse celebrities as Frank Bruno, Bob Monkhouse and Richard Branson.

As 1986 came to an end, Tom had every reason to feel gratified with it. Apart from his youth club work, which he enjoyed, he had bought and renovated a house, improved his painting skill, and been voted a Man of the Year. Then as the year ended came the news that would open a new world for him.

Tom had finally felt confident enough with his painting to submit some examples of his art work to the MFPA. It was evaluated by the panel of experts in Liechtenstein, with the result that he was invited to join the Association.

'When I was told, it was one of the best moments I have ever known,' says Tom today. 'I am so lucky in life and I put it all down to the fact I became a member of the MFPA. Thanks to it, I have everything that able-bodied people take for granted, I have enjoyed a fantastic life as an artist and I have been to places I thought I would never get a chance to see. I still find it all amazing and I am so honoured to be part of such a wonderful organisation.'

Yellow Flowers Watercolour

Tom's involvement with the MFPA has taken him all over the world and brought him into contact with many famous faces.

Clockwise from top left: Tom takes a break during an MFPA convention in Mexico at the Girl Guide World Centre; at an exhibition in Denmark; being interviewed by Sharon Davies; with the Countess of Wessex as she watches MFPA artist David Cawthorne at work; with Rolf Harris at 'Rolf on Art'; with the Mayor of London Boris Johnson and the portrait Tom had painted; presenting a painting to the Right Honourable William Hague MP

Erich Stegmann became a familiar sight in Venice, where he loved to paint

Chapter 9

In order to appreciate how the MFPA was to play such a vital role in shaping Tom's future and establish him as a professional artist, it is necessary to understand the Association's objectives and how it was transformed from a dream to reality by one of the really remarkable men of the 20th century.

The story goes back to the winter of 1912 when a baby boy was born, to the delight of Olga Stegmann and her husband Alois, in the city of Darmstadt. It was the couple's third child and, Herr Stegmann having a good job in a bank, the family enjoyed a contented life in their comfortable home. The baby was christened Arnulf Erich, and it became the custom for him to be called by his second name.

Erich was a happy, healthy baby and it was not until after the Stegmanns moved to Nurnberg in 1914 that he was the cause of parental anxiety by appearing to have a touch of fever. The doctor was called and prescribed medication to bring down the child's temperature. This seemed to be effective until, several days later, Erich suddenly screamed and when his parents rushed to his bedside, they found his small body writhing in agony.

When a paediatrician was called in for a second opinion he found that Erich was suffering with infantile paralysis, as poliomyelitis was called in those days, when it was the fear of parents the world over. He explained there was no treatment for the disease and that paralysis was likely to occur. His prediction proved to be correct; when Erich's agonising back pains and headaches subsided, it was found that he had lost all movement in his hands and arms, and though he could walk it was only for short distances.

He made brave attempts to do everything he could within his limited ability. In this he was encouraged by his parents who had the wisdom not to help him but let him struggle to find ways of doing things by himself. This seemingly hard-hearted policy was to be successfully adopted by Jack and Margaret Yendell years later.

As time passed it became clear that while his body had been cruelly disabled, Erich's mind had not been affected by the virus. At times he suffered from understandable bouts of frustration when he was unable to accomplish some simple task but he never gave up trying to be as independent as possible.

The day that Erich's parents had been dreading came when the little boy had to go to school where he would be surrounded by able-bodied children. He was seated at the back of the class and left to watch his fellow pupils at work. One day when writing materials were being distributed he asked if he could have a piece of paper and a pencil. Bending his head he managed to manoeuvre the end of the pencil so that he could grip it with his teeth. Then he began to print letters, which the children were copying from the blackboard. The teacher was surprised that his attempt was far better than might have been expected.

Later in life Erich explained in an interview, 'I began to write and paint with the other children. They wrote and painted with their hands. My hands, however, were paralysed and I painted with my mouth. I wanted to prove I could do it better than those who were not handicapped and I did.'

His drawing and art work developed so well that when he was 15, he was accepted into art school, and he lived the student life to the full.

He would sit in cafés with friends and lift his glass by holding the rim in his teeth, then tilt his head until the contents trickled into his mouth. It was a technique that Tom has used since he was small.

Apart from the subject of art, politics were endlessly discussed by the students. The country was still reeling from the terrible cost of the so-called Great War and inflation in which a Deutschmark in 1922 became worth less than a hundredth of its 1914 value. In the political spectrum there were various parties, each with a different solution to Germany's problems. These ranged from the Communist Red Veterans' League to the National Socialist Party, abbreviated to the word Nazi. Erich came from a liberal family and his sympathies were firmly with the ordinary folk. Daily on his way to college he saw men as disabled as himself, victims of shellfire rather than a disease, begging in the streets while the stark look of poverty marked more and more faces.

Soon after Erich celebrated his 20th birthday, one of his paintings was exhibited in a Nurnberg Gallery, with the result that he was offered a scholarship from the Albrecht Dürer Foundation, which allowed him to work for a year in the studio of a professional artist of his choice. Erich chose the studio of an artist he greatly admired, the famous Erwin von Kormendy.

'Pictures are like children who leave home. Nobody asks them whether their father has lost a foot or arm.'

After what he later described as one of the happiest years of his life, Erich embarked upon the career of a professional artist. No mention was made of the method he used to paint when his work appeared in galleries, apart from one exception. The owner of a gallery in Italy made a point of impressing his clients by describing how certain pictures on display had been painted by an artist who could not use his hands.

When word of this reached Erich he exploded, 'What difference does it make how a picture is painted? A painter does not mean only a pair of hands – he paints from his heart what his eyes see. Pictures are like children who leave home. Nobody asks them whether their father has lost a foot or arm.'

Today that sentiment remains an article of faith with Tom and his fellow MFPA members.

As Erich's career continued, many of his paintings reflected his attitude towards the prevailing political situation. He had a positive antipathy towards the Nazi regime. Like many disabled people he was conscious of being 'different' and therefore could empathise with those who, because of race, creed or physical handicap, were in danger of being victimised. When one of his 'social' pictures was displayed in an art gallery, pro-Nazi critics condemned it as being decadent.

This criticism gave him great satisfaction as it showed that his 'message' was effective. And apart from his paintings, he never hesitated to proclaim his anti-Nazi views verbally, to the misgiving of his friends. His brother-in-law warned him, 'Sooner or later you will be denounced or in trouble over your paintings.'

Trouble came in 1934 when Erich was arrested and sent to prison as an enemy

Gondolas in Venice Erich Stegmann

of the state. For an able-bodied man to suddenly find himself in gaol is a traumatic experience; for Erich, without the use of his hands, it was devastating.

The cruellest aspect was the rejection of his requests for his paints and brushes, being accused each time of having used them to produce subversive material. Meanwhile his general health was declining alarmingly.

By March of the following year there was still no trial, but on his 24th birthday that same month, Erich was taken before the prison governor.

'The law is being followed correctly,' the official said. 'As there is not enough evidence to convict you, you are free to go but there is a condition – you are forbidden to go back to painting and if you do you will be re-arrested and find yourself in a much worse place than a civil prison.'

It was a stipulation that Erich was to ignore. In order to return to painting where he was less likely to be noticed by the Nurnberg authorities, Erich moved to Deisenhofen, a leafy suburb that lies at the end of the tramline, south of Munich. It had a 'liberal' reputation where Erich believed he was in less danger of being denounced. As it turned out, Deisenhofen was to be his home for the rest of his life. There he began to paint secretly and sell his work 'under the table' to trusted buyers.

This clandestine existence lasted until 1944 when on a winter's day Erich returned home to be warned by a neighbour that a police official has been asking whether she knew if the suspect Stegmann did any painting and if she thought he was loyal to Herr Hitler.

'If he returns, tell him I have gone away – for my health,' Erich told her. Soon he was on his way to the village of St Jodok near the Brenner Pass, only taking his art materials with him. Settling there, he spent his days wandering the countryside and painting in secluded settings. In 1944, word of his activities reached the authorities and he had to go further into hiding.

For Erich, the end of the Second World War meant that he need no longer lead the life of a fugitive, and back in Deisenhofen he set about re-establishing his career as an artist. With the economy shattered by the war, he realised that there was little call for original paintings so he decided to publish some of his pictures as greetings cards. These would sell cheaply and hopefully allied troops stationed in Germany would buy them to send to families and friends.

> He made a point of saying that the project must be run as a business. 'No charity, please,'

When Erich approached a printer, he was told that as a result of the war there was a desperate shortage of card and paper. He would require an official permit to get a necessary supply but this was unlikely for such nonessentials as postcards.

Determined not to be thwarted, he published the world's first wooden postcards. The 'cards', which were crafted by a local carpenter, were the traditional oblong postcard size, two centimetres thick and cut from birch wood. After applying size to prevent paint seeping along the grain, he drew a country scene with a mouth-held pencil and then duly applied the colour.

Although the painting was satisfactory, Erich realised it had taken too long to produce. He therefore decided to start a production line and recruited some local people to help him. His idea was to paint an original 'master' picture, the outlines of which would be copied on to the wooden 'cards' by pencil. Then, rather like 'painting by numbers', the empty spaces would be coloured in, with one person painting the blue of the sky, another the green of the foliage and so on.

The enterprise was highly successful until 1948, when supplies of paper became available in Germany. Erich then set up a new company to produce conventional greetings cards, which continued to be profitable.

****

During his lonely, fugitive days, an idea had grown in Erich's mind and now he felt the time had come to try and make it a reality. In discussing it with a friend he said, 'I am so lucky I can support myself but think about handicapped people like me who have the ability to paint yet have to depend on their families or social security payments to survive.

'While they may be talented, most would need proper tuition to get them up to a professional standard and that is something few could afford.

'I want to form an organisation – an international partnership – of artists who paint either with their mouths or feet.'

Erich went on to explain that the work of those with sufficient artistic ability would be marketed as cards and prints. Everyone would get a share of the proceeds. He made a point of saying that the project must be run as a business. 'No charity, please,' became his dictum.

When the partnership was launched it would need to publish high quality work, so Erich started a Europe-wide quest to find suitable disabled painters to form the nucleus of his proposed group.

The Association of Mouth and Foot Painting Artists (AMFPA) came into being on 19 March 1957, when 16 artists who had been recruited, met at the Waldhotel in Vaduz, Liechtenstein.

'I invited you to become founder members because your work is of a standard that can be published right away,' Erich told them. 'But there are others with the same problems as ourselves who have talent but need help to develop it. It will be the aim of the Association to offer them scholarships so they will be provided with proper materials and tuition until their work reaches a standard for them to become Full Members.

'The Association must run on purely democratic lines. In the future there will be more members in more countries and I propose that members in each region will elect one of their number to represent them on the Board.'

He added that while the Association would be controlled entirely by its members, it would be necessary to employ non-handicapped people to assist in the day-to-day running of the organisation. The essential job of the members would be to paint. The Association's headquarters were established in Liechtenstein because of its political impartiality and the worldwide recognition of the Swiss franc.

Meanwhile the quest for members continued. In 1956 the first English artist was invited to join the fledgling organisation, after a visit by Erich. He was Richard Hext who lived in the village of Ashburton on the edge of Dartmoor. Having been born without the use of his arms, he taught himself to use a mouth-held paintbrush to paint scenic postcards for sale to tourists for a few shillings each in the village shop. On joining the Association, Richard's days of near poverty were over as his work received its true reward.

Another of the early 'discoveries' was Christy Brown. Erich travelled to Ireland to meet him and after seeing his artistic potential invited him to become a member of the Association. Although Christy Brown became world-famous through his autobiography *My Left Foot,* it is not generally known that he was a member of the MFPA until his death in 1981.

He once wrote: 'Painting became the great love in my life, the main pivot of my concentration. I lived in the orbit of my paints and brushes.'

The quest for suitable painters initiated by Erich Stegmann continues today. When contact is made with a disabled person who appears to have artistic potential, he or she is requested to submit examples of their work. If this is judged to show promise, a scholarship is offered which will provide a stipend to cover tuition, painting materials and, where necessary, specialised equipment to meet their particular needs. When a student's work is judged to have reached a certain standard of excellence, that student becomes an Associate Member. The final goal is Full Membership. This is granted when the Association's independent judging panel is satisfied that the work of a mouth or foot painter is equal to that of able-bodied professional artists.

With membership comes a regular income that enables the artist to live free from financial anxiety and concentrate on painting. This income is guaranteed for life even if deteriorating health makes it impossible for the recipient to continue providing pictures for the Association to market in the form of cards, prints and calendars.

This basic rule resulted from Erich Stegmann's deep understanding of how the fear of losing the ability to paint, and with it financial independence, can haunt disabled artists and hinder the creative process.

Another example of Erich's understanding of the handicapped artist's situation was his enthusiasm for members' conventions. Like writers, most artists work by themselves and this can lead to a feeling of isolation. The problem is greater for those who lack the mobility to get out and about like the able-bodied. Thus it was decided early in the history of the Association to arrange meetings where members could get together, make friendships, discuss their work, enjoy visits to renowned art galleries and attend 'workshops' where experts would give helpful advice during painting sessions.

Major cities in different countries have provided venues for these meetings as Erich was a pioneer and champion of 'wheelchair' travel. By arranging these international conventions, the Association helped to bring about the acceptance of the handicapped as travellers.

By the time Erich Stegmann died in 1984, the Association had become established in 37 countries, a figure that is now 76 with nearly 800 members worldwide.

Abstract Watercolour

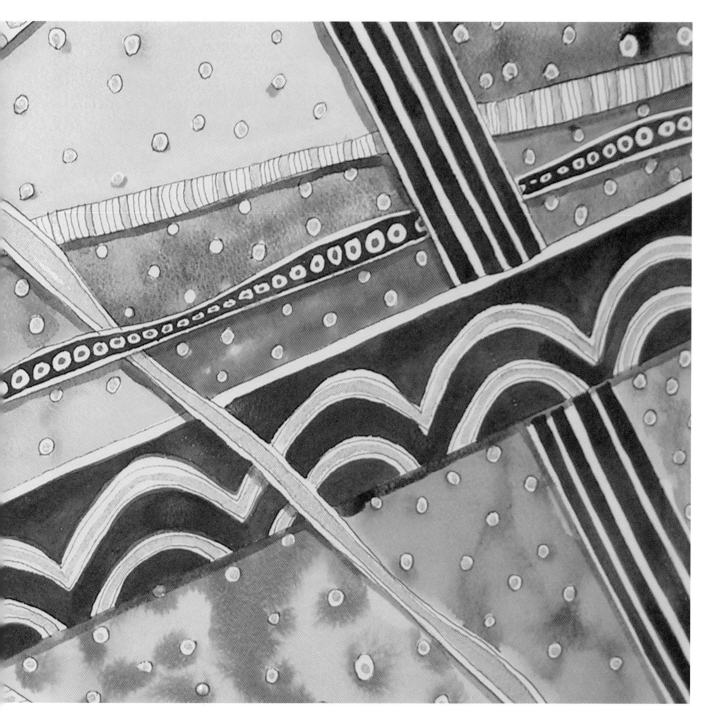

Tom with the painting completed in Mexico City

Chapter 10

The year 1986 had been a very important one for Tom. He had been named a Man of the Year and after hard work he had achieved his ambition of joining the MFPA. The following year promised to be equally eventful. He realised that while he had reached the artistic standard to be accepted as a student, his serious painting career was just beginning if he wanted to attain the status and benefits of Full Membership of the Association. This meant producing work that would be judged equal to that of professional artists who had the use of their arms and hands.

As the MFPA depended on the skill of its members to produce commercial work, Tom was well aware that while he was free to do 'serious' painting, he must also concentrate on pictures that could be turned into greetings cards, calendars and prints. Thus he began painting Christmas cards and while he enjoyed the challenge, he did not find it easy.

Such cards are traditional with snow, holly, robins, Christmas trees and other seasonal symbols. Tom had initial difficulty in portraying the Yuletide atmosphere, especially when painting snow scenes. He was more confident with Father Christmas. Perhaps memory of his father in a Santa costume at Normans Bay had something to do with it.

As he learned more about the workings of the Association Tom, with his penchant for organisation, felt he should like to become involved with such events as exhibitions.

In 1988 Lucy left university with a BA Hons in illustration and graphic design, and at Hunter's Moon she and Tom planned their wedding.

Inevitably some people close to Lucy were worried that by marrying someone with Tom's impairment she might become a permanent carer.

'When you meet someone without arms you wonder how well they can manage,' Lucy says, adding with a laugh, 'It was awful when someone would pat Tom on the head. But he could dress himself, cook, drive a car and do nearly all the things able-bodied people do and there was never a problem except he deplored the fact that he could not do up the top button of his shirt.

'We decided to get married on 8 August 1988, so with the date of 8.8.88 Tom has no excuse for forgetting our anniversary.'

The wedding was held in a very pretty, very old little village church close to Hunter's Moon and it was an especially happy occasion.

'It was the last time all the family was together,' says Tom. 'Both our grandmothers were there, my sister Adrienne came from Jordan and my brother David flew from Australia to be best man.'

Like Tom's parents in their courtship days, he and Lucy had not been able to spend much time together and now they were determined that their wedding would be a real celebration. And it was. The bride in a white wedding dress and holding a bouquet of pink roses was driven to the church by her father in his vintage drophead Jowett Jupiter. Tom was waiting in a grey morning suit complete with matching top hat.

The wedding breakfast was worthy of the effort that had been put into it. The groom's father excelled himself by providing a beautifully decorated, blue-and-white iced cake that the guests agreed was sensational.

When Tom and Lucy describe their wedding to friends one question is invariably asked of Tom, 'How did you manage about the ring?'

Tom smiles ruefully and Lucy explains, 'I had to put it on my finger

Tom and Lucy were married on Monday 8th August 1988 so that, according to Lucy, Tom has no excuse for forgetting their anniversary

myself. As for our honeymoon I had always been fascinated by the thought of Iceland so we went there. I had to persuade Tom who was not so keen on the idea but he liked it when we got there.'

When it comes to holidays Lucy enjoys cool climates while Tom is happier in high temperatures, saying that his body seems to work best in warm conditions. But both are tolerant and these differences have never affected their mutual enjoyment of travel.

'I found Iceland to be fascinating,' says Tom. 'We were booked on a tour as it is best to go into the interior with someone who can drive off-road. We visited amazing waterfalls, hot springs and geysers, and the site of the Althing which, going back 1,000 years, was the world's first parliament.'

> Being sent to Treloars was one of the best things that ever happened to him.

In Reykjavik Tom was interviewed by the Press as he was regarded as a novelty. Not only was he without arms but he could paint – and he was on his honeymoon! Good newspaper material.

'I was so impressed by the Icelanders' attitude towards the disabled,' he says. 'They have a Union of Disabled People which owns a specially designed building where the handicapped can rent apartments. There is a gym, swimming pool, craft room, its own taxi service and a "bank" of carers.'

After Tom and Lucy returned to England they settled down to life at Hunter's Moon. Lucy took a job as a designer with a packaging firm and Tom worked in his studio. To watch him putting paint on canvas is fascinating but equally intriguing is to watch him select a tube of paint from the array near his feet, unscrew the cap, squeeze paint on to a palette and mix the colours until he has the exact shade he needs – all with his toes.

While Tom was happy to have a studio of his own to work in, he did find one drawback. He is a gregarious person and found the lack of company a problem.

Speaking of those days in Hunter's Moon Lucy says, 'Tom started off painting at home but he just could not do it. He needs interaction with others.'

In 1989 the situation improved when Tom returned to Treloars to take up the new position of part-time activities co-ordinator. With the expansion of the college it had been decided that it would be fitting to have a disabled person in this role, and who more suited for it than Tom Yendell. It certainly suited him because it allowed him enough time to continue with his art work.

* * * *

In 1989 Tom and Lucy exchanged Hunter's Moon for a new house in the village of Holybourne, near Alton, where they still reside. The reason for the move was that their new home was close to Treloar College which made life easier. Tom was happy to be associated with the school again. It had meant so much to him in his formative years, especially in his art work, thanks to his late mentor Alyn Wilde. As he has said, being sent to Treloars was one of the best things that ever happened to him. What he enjoyed about his work was that it provided an outlet for his organising ability which is such a vital part of his make-up.

This aspect was also evident in his relationship with the MFPA. Apart from painting for the Association, he wanted to contribute to it. Being mobile and able to drive his own car, he felt he would be able to assist with exhibitions and similar events. But, remembering Erich Stegmann's axiom 'No charity please', there would be no question of fundraising.

Tom has remarked how fortunate he is that he has the normal use of his legs; that he can walk without difficulty and is therefore able to do things that many other members of the Association are incapable of doing. He often thought of those who are housebound and find painting a lonely occupation.

The more he mused about it, the more an idea began to form, but that would be something for the future – in 1990, he and Lucy were looking forward to the birth of their first child.

They could not help being anxious because at that time, there was fear that defects caused by thalidomide could be inherited.

'Before the birth, we went to a thalidomide meeting,' says Lucy. 'There was a professor there who explained that there was no way possible there could be genetic problems. We were very, very reassured and when I had a scan we saw that the baby was all there!'

Tom and Lucy set about decorating a bedroom specially for the baby, who arrived two weeks ahead of schedule on 7 January 1991, just three days after his room had been completed.

Tom playing with his son Joe

Tom, who was present at the birth, was ecstatic at the arrival of his son who was to be christened Joseph.

'It's so exciting but you suddenly realise that life is never going to be the same again,' said Tom as he took on the role of fatherhood.

Understandably people have remarked how sad it must have been for Tom not being able to embrace the baby or pick him up but this problem was soon solved. When Tom needed to carry him, little Joseph was laid in a towel which Tom gripped with his teeth and thus lifted him without difficulty. He would also lie on his back and, holding Joseph with his feet, play with him as happily as any able-bodied father.

As Joseph grew older, he was so used to Tom's impairment that he seemed to be unaware of it. Lucy tells how once the family were at a Thalidomide Society event where Tom was playing pool with another thalidomider. Suddenly Joseph whispered to her, 'Look Mum, there's a man over there who hasn't got any arms.'

'Well, he's like your dad,' she replied.

'What!' cried Joseph. He gazed at Tom and exclaimed, 'Dad, you haven't got any arms!'

When Joseph went to school he might have been teased about having an armless father but when his classmates saw him arrive by car they acclaimed Tom as 'cool' because he could drive without the use of his hands.

Tom and Lucy were so happy and thankful for Joseph's safe arrival they decided that, as a token of gratitude, they would sponsor an African child who would not have the advantages that their child could expect. They continued their sponsorship for a number of years which maintained their interest in the plight of deprived African children. As it was to turn out, it was a prophetic gesture.

✳✳✳✳

For some time Tom had been thinking about an idea to put to the MFPA. It was to have a permanent gallery for its members' work. Apart from displaying their paintings and holding special exhibitions, it would be a focal point where those members with mobility could meet to discuss their work and socialise. And it would be of interest to members of the public who knew about the Association through buying greetings cards, to see full-sized original paintings and on occasion watch mouth and foot artists demonstrating their techniques.

The more Tom considered the idea, the more enthusiastic he

became. The question to which he had no immediate answer was where such a gallery should be located.

Returning one day from visiting his parents in Bexhill, Tom drove through the village of Selborne, which is close to Holybourne. He jammed on his brakes when he saw there was a 'For Sale' sign on an old antiques shop. He said to Lucy, 'That would make a fantastic gallery.'

The next day he was in touch with the Association's London office and the publisher came to Selborne to see what Tom was so excited about.

Tom believed that Selborne would be an ideal setting for what he had in mind. A great number of visitors came to the village that was originally made famous by Gilbert White, the clergyman-naturalist whose *Natural History and Antiquities of Selborne* was published in 1789. The book became an English classic and White's house, known as The Wakes, is now a museum dedicated to him. On its upper floors,

MFPA artists gathered for the opening of the gallery in Selborne in 1992

memorabilia of Lawrence Oates, who died on Scott's expedition to the South Pole, and the African explorer Frank Oates, is on display.

After due consideration the MFPA bought the shop and Tom set to work to transform it into an attractive art gallery. At times assisted by Lucy, he would be both curator and resident artist so that visitors would not only see original work by the Association's members but also would be able to watch it being painted 'without hands'.

The gallery was formally opened at the end of October 1992 by Lord

Selborne who declared, 'The gallery is for artists who, whatever their disabilities, are professional painters and want to be treated as such.' And the point was made that the gallery was dedicated to exhibiting the work of all disabled artists, not just those of the Association.

The local press reported that 'more than 40 pictures are on display at the gallery, including four striking works by the Association's founder Erich Stegmann.' And when Tom was interviewed he said, 'I am a great believer that art is in the heart and the head, not in the hands.'

Speaking later about the gallery's early days Tom said, 'We used to get the benefit of visitors coming to see Gilbert White's village. Now people come specially to visit the gallery. It also acts as a base from which we organise talks on the work of the Association. Schools and bodies such as Rotary Clubs and the WI that would like to have a speaker from the MFPA can contact us there.

'One of the great advantages of Selborne is that it is close to Treloar College, where MFPA artists get together for several days each year while the regular students are on holiday. They have workshops on painting and come to the gallery where special exhibitions are arranged. This gives them a chance to see the work of others and their own pictures displayed for public viewing. Similar exhibitions for all artists have been held at Winchester and London.'

✴✴✴✴

The opening of the Selborne Gallery was a triumph for Tom. He saw his idea become a reality and he greatly relishes such episodes. And no doubt in his art work he experiences a similar sense of gratification, when a mental image is transformed on to canvas as a consummate painting.

The gallery meant that Tom's days were busier than ever, but at least while he was 'minding the shop', he was able to continue with his painting in an adjoining studio. Seeing an MFPA painter at work was an extra attraction for visitors. But there was much else to do. Customers had to be attended to when they bought cards and prints, and they asked questions about the Association and the artists whose work was on display.

There was also the organising of special exhibitions. Sometimes this included the work of foreign artists which meant pictures being obtained from abroad. Tom did have help, particularly from Lucy and a picture framer named Roger Saunders, who framed large prints and original paintings for the Association.

Apart from the satisfaction of running the gallery, Tom found that he was increasingly involved with the MFPA and his fellow artists. In the course of time he became an unofficial mentor to new members, always ready to offer good-humoured advice and practical solutions to their problems when he received anxious telephone calls. He was also instrumental in helping some potential students to be considered for MFPA membership.

An example of this was described to the author by Katrina Gardner. Due to thalidomide, she had also been born without arms though she has hands where, under normal circumstances, her arms would join her shoulders. Such hands are referred to by thalidomiders as 'flippers'.

While still a baby Katrina would be set down on the floor surrounded by coloured pencils and, like Tom, she began using her toes to doodle with them. It was not until her first day at school that she realised she was different from the other children. Because she was an easy target, she was bullied in the playground so she was enrolled in a special school for the handicapped.

'I loved that school because it seemed natural for everyone to have some disability, and we were always there for each other,' Katrina said.

When she was 21 she married, and had four children. When her marriage ended, she found that apart from the difficulties of single parenthood, there was the added problem of her disability, yet she managed. When her children needed bathing she would put them in the bath and wash them with her feet.

Tom has been instrumental in encouraging Katrina Gardner to follow a career as an artist

As the children became more self-reliant Katrina was able to join an art class held in a village hall near her home at Sproatley, in Humberside. Having no difficulty in using a pencil with her foot, she hoped it might be possible to manipulate a paintbrush.

When friends saw her first completed picture they exclaimed in surprise, 'Did you really do that?' Their words could not have been more encouraging. One of her pictures depicted Captain Cook's ship *Endeavour* and she proudly hung it in her living room.

When she needed to have work done on her house she engaged an architect who specialised in designing kitchens for thalidomiders.

'When he saw my painting, he asked if I was a member of the MFPA,' Katrina recalls. 'I said I wasn't and did not know much about it. He said he would have a word with a man called Tom Yendell, which he did.

'Soon I got a phone call from Tom

who asked if I painted with my feet. When I said I did he asked, "Could I possibly come and see you. Have everything laid out so I can see you paint."

'He drove up from Hampshire and after I demonstrated how I worked, he took away six of my paintings to present to the MFPA. The result was that I was taken on as a student. It is a wonderful organisation and it is lovely to be a part of it, like being a member of a family of artists. Tom impressed upon me that if I needed assistance or advice I could always turn to him and it is reassuring to know that he is always there.'

Other artists tell of similar support.

****

Erich Stegmann was an enthusiastic traveller. In setting up the MFPA he journeyed to various parts of Western Europe in search of disabled people with artistic talent to join his fledgling organisation. It was not only necessary, it was something that gave him great pleasure despite the fact that travel for the disabled was not as easy in his day as now. He was an advocate for proper travel facilities for the handicapped, especially as the Association's far-flung conventions required members, many in wheelchairs, to make long air journeys.

It was not only business that caused him to travel; his desire to paint new scenes lured him to many exotic locations in different parts of the world, as his paintings testify. Tom found that in a number of ways he followed in the footsteps of Erich Stegmann, and in particular, shared his love of travel.

This wanderlust began some time before he joined the MFPA, with a visit to Australia where his brother David was working.

'I was 16 and it was the first time I had ever been abroad on my own so it was an exciting trip,' Tom says. 'My brother had been in Australia for a year. He married Jan, an Australian girl, and my parents went out for the wedding. When they came back they suggested that I went out there for Christmas. I flew with QANTAS and in those days it took 24 hours. We stopped at Bombay for a couple of hours and the interior of the plane was sprayed with insecticide.

'I was looked after so well by the air hostesses that I did not have any difficulties.'

When he arrived in Perth, Tom's problem was that it was the hottest summer on record and he was wearing warm trousers, his school blazer and a cap suitable for an English winter.

Tom explains that not having arms he has less body surface to release the heat and he was sweltering. David had to rush him to a shop and fit him out with a wardrobe of light summer clothing.

'That journey gave me my love of flying and travel,' says Tom. 'Experiencing different customs and cultures and getting to know different people is really exciting.'

When one listens to Tom talking about incidents in his life, it would be understandable to think that because he is able to travel and do many of the things that come naturally to able-bodied people, he finds it all relatively easy. That is not the case. Tom's life has been a chain of challenges, ranging from trying to draw with a crayon between his toes to learning to drive.

Even tasks that are so simple for most of us, that we do them without thinking, have presented a challenge to Tom. For instance, how would one pull up one's trousers without hands? In this case Tom's solution is simple but effective – a short length of dowelling with a cup hook at one end. Pressing the other end tightly under his chin he bends, manoeuvres the hook into a belt loop and straightens up pulling the trousers into position.

Such is Tom's nature that as he has grown older he welcomes

challenges. In modern parlance they give him a buzz. And without doubt travel – especially by himself – has had its quota of challenges.

****

While at Treloars Tom went with a college party to Switzerland and soon he found a challenge to contest. In Gstaad he watched as his friends were introduced to skiing and as they learned to glide down the nursery slopes he was filled with the ambition to do likewise. No doubt the instructor had his doubts as the skis were strapped on to Tom's feet but Tom was adamant.

'It was marvellous,' he says. 'I even enjoyed falling over in the snow.'

Not being able to use ski poles to steer and balance, he had to control everything by body movement, as he did when riding his specially adapted bicycle. But despite plenty of tumbles he could ski by the time he returned to England, and skiing remains one of his favourite holiday recreations.

Tom skiing In Gstaad

Tom's travels were often more than holidays, being connected with his work. When he returned to Treloar College as activities co-ordinator he and an art teacher took a group of students to Israel.

'At that point I had met Lucy who is a vegan and does not eat any animal products at all,' says Tom. 'I was madly in love and told her when I was going to Israel that I would not eat meat and so when I went there I lived on barbecued vegetables and rice.'

The visit did not start well for him.

'At the place where we stayed in Jerusalem, they had not told us they had put chlorine in the swimming pool and when I went for a swim I got chlorine poisoning,' he recalls. 'I slept for two days before they could wake me up.

'One day we set out to visit a kibbutz, on which was a huge chicken farm. As we drove up to it we saw there was a massive bonfire ahead. We got out of the coach and the head of the kibbutz told he was really sorry but there was nothing to see because the previous night the air conditioning units had broken down in the chicken huts and they had all suffocated. There were thousands of dead chickens on the bonfire.

'I went and looked around and found that each chicken had spent its life in a cage equivalent in size to a shoe box. That made me become a vegetarian permanently.'

❋❋❋❋

After the MFPA gallery was opened in Selborne, Tom's hours were crowded. Apart from time devoted to the gallery as its curator, there were other calls on his time. As a result of interest taken in the gallery, now mentioned in a guidebook to the village, Tom was invited to give talks on the work of the MFPA, in which he demonstrated his own painting technique. This continues, with him averaging 25 talks a year and organising four or five exhibitions. But

Family life is vitally important to Tom and however busy his life gets, he has always made time for his children Joe and Holly

whatever the pressure of work, two things remained sacrosanct. One was 'quality time' with little Joseph because Tom and Lucy believed that time is the best gift one can give a child. The other was when Tom settled down with a drawing board at his feet and painted in the hope of becoming a Full Member of the MFPA.

Over the years he had painted mainly by mouth. He had tried a variety of pigments and a wide range of subjects which now included scenes for greetings cards. As a child he had used his toes to paint but later he took to mouth painting as he felt it gave him slightly more control. But like other mouth painters he found it could present a problem.

When he was working on the large mural at Treloar College he painted by mouth and the work was almost finished when he fell ill and was hurried to hospital with a mystery complaint. Soon it was realised that the cause of the ailment was due to the fact that for three days he had been applying paint with a mouth-held brush and, with it so close to his face, he had been breathing in paint and turpentine fumes.

After that he preferred to use his foot, though at times he still mouth-paints with watercolours for certain pictures, especially those with floral subjects.

Since Tom became an artist he has experimented with various methods of painting and a while ago he found what for him was the ideal – painting on silk.

He explains, 'With silk you draw your image on paper to start with, then you lay the paper behind the fabric and use it like tracing paper, which means you can get the image correct on paper before you start painting. You work with a wooden frame that stretches the silk taut.'

Tom uses gutta to outline the configuration of his proposed picture with fine lines. Colours are then applied to the areas bounded by these lines which prevent the paint from seeping along the silk fibres. The

Exotic Flowers Silk Painting

Abstract Silk Painting

results are highly effective, as illustrations in this book prove.

Tom's mother was particularly interested in Tom's silk paintings because as a girl she had worked in the silk printing department of a printing company.

'Try everything' is Tom's motto and it applies to his art as well as to so many things in his crowded life. As a change from painting he decided to try metal sculpture. First he sketched out what he had in mind and then drew its outlines on sheet metal. As he was unable to go further his nephew, a welder, cut the metal into the required shapes and then welded them together. Tom had his first three-dimensional work of art.

✻✻✻✻

On one occasion Tom took on the role of a model rather than the artist. The statue of the MFPA artist Alison Lapper by renowned British sculptor Marc Quinn had become famous when it won the contest to be set up on the fourth plinth – the 'empty plinth' – in Trafalgar Square.

Marc Quinn was responsible for seven other statues of people with arms or legs missing so that they appeared like classic statues whose limbs had been damaged by the passage of time. One of these was Tom. The sculpting process required him to have a plaster cast made of his body which revived

Tom views the marble statue of himself by the artist Marc Quinn, which was on display in Covent Garden

childhood memories of hot plaster of Paris bandages and their smell being applied when his artificial arms were being designed.

When the statue Tom Yendell was completed in 2003, it was displayed in London's Victoria and Albert Museum and then in various galleries abroad, until it finally came to rest in an American collection. Tom says it was a very strange experience when he first saw his naked replica in white marble.

****

The year 1995 was a special one for Tom and Lucy with the arrival of a daughter whom they named Holly and who today shows signs of inheriting her father's and mother's artistic ability.

The following year was also special. Tom was informed that as his painting had reached the required high standard, he was now a Full Member of the MFPA. It was certainly a time for celebration as it not only meant that his talent had been recognised and he would have the security of a regular income for life, but also that he had earned the status of being a professional artist.

One of the great advantages of being a member of the Association is being able to visit the international conferences, which are held in different cities from time to time. Erich Stegmann's idea of disabled artists from various countries getting together, was something that Tom hugely enjoys. Not only has he visited places he might not otherwise have reached, but he has also made friends with fellow MFPA artists from different parts of the world.

An example of this occurred when he was at an MFPA convention in Mexico City.

'At this meeting students were invited as well as members and there was a beautiful girl of maybe 13 who, having no arms, was a mouth painter,' Tom says. 'She was wearing a smart button-up jacket, jeans and

Tom feeding Holly

fashionable trainers. She had come with her parents from an Amazon village and I was the first person she had met who was armless like her. Not knowing the language they speak in Amazonia I could not communicate with them until I found an interpreter.

'"How independent is she?" I asked the mother. She told me that they had to do everything for her.

'"If she wears trainers she cannot use her feet and will always have to rely on you," I told her. 'Let her learn to use her toes and wear loose clothes that she can put on and off by herself."'

On the last day of the convention the girl's father told Tom they were taking his advice and having seen how he managed to cope with his disability, they realised it might be possible for their daughter to look after herself. Tom felt he had played the role of Dr Wilkie who had shown his mother and father that it is possible to be independent without arms.

Tom and Lucy with AMFPA president Eros Bonamini and his wife Giuseppina at the 50th anniversary in Vienna

Of all the conventions that Tom has attended, the one that impressed him most was held in Vienna.

'All artists were invited to do a painting for the exhibition celebrating 50 years of the MFPA,' Tom explains. 'It was an incredible anniversary. A hundred artists were invited, 90 of them in wheelchairs. The organisation was marvellous with translators and medical staff standing by.

'It opened with a trip down the Danube and the gala dinner was an amazing event in a magnificent hall with round tables, each with a candelabra. The waiters wore powdered wigs and knickerbockers that were fashionable in Mozart's day. And we had the Vienna Royal Philharmonic Orchestra with a couple of opera singers to entertain us. Best of all, we felt we were part of a big happy family.'

****

In 1997 Tom and Lucy decided to spend some time with Tom's brother David in Australia 'before the kids got too old and settled in school.' David lived in a coastal town named Albany, in Western Australia, where he worked as a probation officer. Apart from the attraction of a family holiday, Tom had a second reason for making the trip – he wanted to tackle his greatest challenge ever.

The problem of leaving the Selborne gallery for a long period was solved when his parents agreed to look after it in his absence.

Then there was the question of transport in Australia. David had his daily work to do so Tom could not expect to be

Tom with fellow MFPA artists at the convention in Vienna. From left: Kris Kirk, David Cawthorne, Keith Jansz, Steven Chambers and Alison Lapper

chauffeured everywhere. He therefore arranged to have his car shipped out. The cost would be less than hiring a car for the time they planned to be there and anyway he doubted if it would be possible to hire a suitably adapted vehicle.

Tom had owned a couple of cars since his first Mini Clubman and his current motor was a bright red Jeep, with a soft top.

Tom and the family in the red Jeep they took with them on their trip to Australia

'I decided I would take the foot-steering Jeep,' he says. 'I'd had it for about three years. It had belonged to a man who was wheelchair-bound and who had this Jeep specially designed for him. It was originally a Ford Cortina car that had been converted to look like an American army Jeep – rather different from the Mini or the Escort I'd had.

'All the adaptations were on the floor, and the speedometer and dials were low down as well. In the summer when I had the top down and drove up to traffic lights, lorries would often come alongside and the drivers would look down at me and then do a double take when they saw there was no steering wheel!'

One of the main reasons why Tom was eager to go to Australia was to take up scuba diving – not an easy sport for someone without arms but something he had long been determined to try.

'My brother had told me there was a diving club in Albany,' Tom explains, 'He had said to them, "My brother wants to learn to dive," and was told "Bring him in." When he told them about my condition the instructor, Ron Moore, said, "If he doesn't mind going underwater I'd love to try and teach him."'

Tom has said that what he likes about Australians is that they speak their minds and are quite open about disability, sometimes with a hint of what some might regard as Aussie humour.

'I remember the first weekend we were there and I hadn't really met any Australians. There was an open day at the local vineyard, so we went. As we got out of the car this guy came over to me. He'd obviously had a few drinks. He looked me up and down and said, "Flamin' heck, mate, I can understand you losing one but how the hell did you manage two!"'

Soon after Tom and Lucy arrived in Australia, David arranged for them to go to a factory to have Tom's wetsuit made.

'A young woman came out to measure me up and then worked out the price,' Tom recalls with a grin. 'I cheekily said, "As I haven't any arms there won't be any sleeves in my wetsuit so obviously it will be a lot cheaper."

'Without blinking she turned around and said, "No mate, with a bum the size of yours it will be twice as expensive."

When the wetsuit was ready, they all went down to the seashore for Tom to try it out. He walked into the water and, with Lucy and the two children waving him on, waded out until he was up to his neck. Then he turned and saw their cheerful waving had changed and they were pointing out to sea with worried faces.

'I turned round and I saw a big triangular fin moving through the water,' Tom says. 'Lucy said she had never seen me move so quickly. I was out like a shot. My brother laughed and said the shark probably thought I was a seal in my wetsuit with my legs flipping and no arms.'

At the diving school Tom had his first lessons in the swimming pool. He has enjoyed swimming ever since he was a little boy and David pushed him into a school pool. What Tom found rewarding about swimming was that it gave him the sensation of physical equality with the able-bodied.

Now he had to demonstrate to his instructor that he could swim and this he did by swimming a full length underwater.

'I had to learn about the routine details of scuba diving – the air gauge and so on,' Tom says. 'And I knew it would be the one time in my life when I would have to rely on other people. Because divers go down in pairs, I not only had to have a "buddy", but he had to have one as well in case anything went wrong. I did not count as one of a pair.

'We had all sorts of problems, the biggest was to do with communication which is done between divers by hand signals.'

Tom getting to grips with the scuba gear at the diving school

The answer was for Tom and his buddy to have special full-faced masks, each with an inbuilt microphone and earpiece. When they spoke the sound waves were transmitted through the water to each other.

Tom prepared for his first dive with an air cylinder strapped on his back. No doubt it brought back a childhood memory of wearing gas cylinders to power his prosthetic arms.

'After I had done all my tests, my first dive was in open sea and the instructor said we would go down about 12 feet to begin with,' Tom remembers. 'When we were at the bottom a shadow appeared over our heads and I looked up to see an enormous stingray. It was the size of a double bed.'

The effect on Tom's breathing was dramatic but to his great relief the creature swam away. When they got back on land Tom said to the instructor, 'Did you see that! It was massive!'

'You don't need to worry about him,' he replied. 'That's old Jake. He was caught about 14 years ago and the fishermen cut off his sting. Now the divers feed him by hand and he's quite tame.'

What Tom particularly liked about diving was the brilliantly coloured fish that darted about him. Needless to say such underwater scenes have inspired his silk painting.

Tom loved scuba diving, despite the communication difficulties, and having to go down with a dive buddy who needed his own dive buddy

During the family's visit to Australia Joseph attended a local school and Holly went to a play group. Tom received invitations to give talks on the MFPA to Rotary Clubs and the Women's Guild. After one such evening a lady from the local services approached him and said that one of her clients who had cerebral palsy had always wanted to drive but had never been able to find someone who could adapt a vehicle for him. Would Tom be willing to sell his adapted car to him when he returned to England?

'We took him to the shore when the tide was out so he could try driving the red Jeep,' says Tom. 'He took to it like a duck to water and social services paid me the amount it had cost me to export it to Australia. I think he was able to drive it for five or six years so it was nice to see how it helped somebody else.'

Lucy had long had a wish to visit New Zealand and, as ever eager to see vistas new, they made a flying visit there. The high spot of their trip was Rotorua, a town in the North Island which is noted for its sulphurous aroma due to its famous hot springs and geysers jetting great columns of scalding water and steam into the atmosphere, like the ones they had seen in Iceland.

Shortly before it was time to return to England, Tom and David went to Bali. Reminiscing about the trip Tom says, 'I got to love Bali. I loved the people and I loved the food and the temperature as my body works a lot better when I am in a warm climate. We stayed in the main city and then went up to the north of the island. I met Andrew Baker, a mouth-painting artist, who lived there. After I told him about the MFPA he subsequently joined the Association and has been with us for quite a few years.'

While Tom was in Bali a leather worker designed a special wallet for him that he now wears strapped to his right ankle. Until then he had a bag with a shoulder strap to hold the articles that men usually carry in their pockets but it was not easy to use, especially when he had to get money out of it. With the ankle wallet he easily selects the notes he requires with the toes of his left foot. If he receives coins in his change, they are deposited in one of his shoes, which are designed to slip on and off without difficulty.

When Tom left Australia he had achieved his long-held ambition to gain a PADI certificate endorsing him as a fully qualified scuba diver. It has been said of him that he is possibly the only armless person in the world to have this qualification.

Over the years Tom has become proficient at horse riding, skiing and scuba diving but there is still a sporting challenge he intends to meet. That is to step out of an aeroplane to make a tandem parachute jump.

✳✳✳✳

On returning from Australia Tom found himself more occupied than ever with the Selborne gallery, exhibitions, talks and, of course, painting. And it was not long before he found another outlet for his energy. In company with the well-known mouth painters Trevor Wells and Keith Jansz, he became a trustee for the MFPA Trust Fund for Training Handicapped Children in the Arts.

The name is self-explanatory and it is financed by donations and legacies. Grants are made to disabled children either singly or to schools, drama groups and suchlike bodies.

'Most of our grants go to individual children who want to do an art course or learn music and need specific instruments,' Tom explains. 'We concentrate on children with physical disabilities in the hope that we will find some new mouth painters.'

The Trust also organised a fun competition known as 'Baa-Art' aimed at getting disabled children interested in drawing and painting. An outline of a sheep was printed on both sides of A3 sheets of paper. These were posted to 350 special schools for children to decorate and return to the MFPA. A judging panel selected the best ten entries and the winners received a full-sized fibreglass cast of a sheep on which to paint their designs. These colourful creatures were first displayed at an MFPA exhibition in Winchester's Great Hall.

As the year 2000 approached, Holybourne Village Association decided that the millennium should be commemorated by a permanent memorial. This was to take the form of two mosaic panels, one showing a plan of the area as it was 2,000 years ago, when it was a crossing point of two Roman roads that linked Winchester and London, and Silchester and Chichester. The other panel depicts aspects of the present-day village. The panels are now mounted on the wall of the village hall.

The artist who designed and fabricated these mosaics was Lucy Yendell and needless to say Tom was very proud of her.

Tom celebrated his 40th birthday in 2002, which held very special significance for him.

'Thalidomiders were not meant to live to 40,' he explains. 'The drug manufacturer's medical experts said we were not going to live beyond that age so they could keep the compensation down. And the parents of the 1,500 thalidomide babies which did not survive, received no compensation at all. The curious thing is that those of us who did survive appear to have a slightly higher life expectancy than normal.'

Despite so much of his time being taken up by work, Tom's travelling days were far from over, especially thanks to the MFPA conventions that have been held from time to time in various countries since they were inaugurated by Erich Stegmann. Thus in 2002 he took part in an international conference in Madrid, where he renewed friendships with fellow artists from various countries.

Tom and Lucy also found time to take Joe and Holly on a family holiday in Mauritius.

'It was a great experience,' Tom recalls. 'On the second day, there

Tom with the Countess of Wessex viewing the winners of the MFPA Trust Fund 'Baa-Art' competition on display in Winchester's Great Hall in Hampshire

we were swimming in the sea when Lucy said, "Look at those guys over there." A group of four young men were standing around our belongings which we had left on the beach. It was a little worrying and she thought she would see what they were up to. As she waded ashore one of them, pointing at me still in the water, asked, "Is that your friend?"

'"That's my husband!" she answered.

'One of the young men said, "My friend would like to meet him. He's a guy with no arms."

'So we met this young Mauritian who had lost his arms through being accidentally electrocuted and I was the first person he had seen in the same condition. He somehow bought and sold things at the market.

'His friends, in their early 20s, were lovely. They said, "Have you been around our island?" After we shook our heads they took us all over and introduced us to their families. We were invited to have Christmas dinner with one.

'There is a mouth painter in Mauritius called Stephanie Couronne and we went to visit her at her parents' home. She was so overwhelmed because until then she had never met any other mouth and foot artists. So that was a bonus.'

The high spot of Tom's year was in July when word went round Selborne that a member of the royal family would

HRH The Prince of Wales visited the gallery on the occasion of its 10th anniversary. His Royal Highness is seen here watching MFPA artist Robert Trent at work while Tom looks on

On his visit to the Selborne gallery, Prince Charles was presented with a painting by Trevor Wells (seated right). On the left is MFPA artist Keith Jansz

be making an appearance in the village. The occasion was the opening of The Wakes Field Centre. It was also the tenth anniversary of the opening of the MFPA gallery and Prince Charles took the opportunity to visit it.

He was welcomed by Tom, who was remembered from his days as a photographer with Business in the Community, one of the Prince's charities.

Robert Trent, a Student Member of the Association, demonstrated mouth painting to the Prince who is a keen artist himself; he has exhibited at the Royal Academy under the name of 'Arthur George Carrick'; a reference to his official title which includes Earl of Carrick. He therefore showed discerning interest in the techniques used by MFPA artists to produce the pictures on display and in discussing art with Trevor Wells and Keith Jansz, who were also present.

Tom could not have had a better token of appreciation for his efforts to establish a gallery devoted to the work of his fellow artists.

The fact that people enjoyed looking at the work of MFPA painters was proved by the success of the Selborne gallery.

'We were invited to do some outdoor exhibitions,' says Tom. 'We used to put up a tent with boards, on which to display the pictures. Then we were given a stand at the annual Mobility Road Show. It was all to do with mobility but they used to have other things to get people interested. As it became more and more popular it spread and eventually there was no room for us.

'We were offered a space outside on the grass and we used a marquee, which took four guys to erect it and later take it down. The problem with marquees is that they are not very good for pictures, especially when it is windy and the display boards flap.'

On one occasion, Tom was walking round the site of the show looking at a line of parked exhibition trailers which

Tom presenting his painting of Westminster Abbey to HRH The Duke of Edinburgh at the Mobility Roadshow

were being opened up. It gave him an idea. What was needed was a converted trailer to replace the marquee. He searched the internet and found a company in Chichester that specialised in exhibition trailers.

The project found favour and work began on what was to be a mobile art gallery.

Tom says, 'Before it was converted, it was an old mobile burger bar or something like that, but we stripped it out completely so that there was enough room to display 60 pictures. Demonstrations of mouth and foot painting could take place under an extending canopy.

'We take it to county shows and civic places, so that the public can see that we are real people who actually paint with their mouths and feet. In the first year we went to Winchester, Cirencester, the Surrey County Show, Trafalgar Square and the Greenbelt Christian Festival.'

Sometimes there is a last-minute invitation to some event to replace an exhibitor who has dropped out. The advantage of the trailer is that when this happens the travelling gallery is always ready for immediate use.

The MFPA's mobile exhibition trailer helps to spread the word about the Association's work.

Madam Hannah and the sewing and textiles class: part of the TEABAG project

Chapter 11

It was the sight of a tall Englishman dressed in the colourful robes of an African chief, complete with a headdress of feathers, that heralded what was to become one of the most enriching chapters in Tom's life. The year was 2005 and the scene was the Congress Theatre in Eastbourne where a Rotary Club conference was being held. There was also an exhibition of MFPA paintings, hence Tom's presence.

Unable to curb his curiosity Tom went up to the figure in the exotic costume and asked, 'Why are you dressed like this?'

'I am the chairman of TEABAG,' was the bewildering reply. The idea of a teabag having a chairman seemed so extraordinary that Tom's expression was one of amused bewilderment.

'I must explain,' said the tall man who introduced himself as Roger Gillman. 'TEABAG stands for The Education and Book Appeal Ghana, and we use the acronym because it sticks in people's minds.' He added that he was dressed as an African chief as a gimmick to promote his charity.

Tom had been interested in Africa and African children ever since he and Lucy had sponsored an African child as a thanksgiving gesture, following the birth of their son Joseph in 1991. So he asked Roger to tell him the TEABAG story. Roger, who explained he was an undertaker in South London where a number of Ghanaian people live, was happy to oblige.

'It all goes back to 2002 when I went to Ghana on business,' he said. 'One day I was being driven along the coast road and, having time on my hands, I asked the driver to take me to some place where I could have a swim. He took me down a side road to a seaside village named Mankoadze.

'I immediately fell in love with the village and its people, so much so, that although I had originally gone to Ghana for a week I stayed on in Mankoadze for a few extra days. There I met the local hierarchy including Nana George – the word 'Nana' means king – and the Queen Mother, both being tribal leaders.

Tom with TEABAG chairman Roger Gillman (left) and Castro Amoah, the TEABAG college principal

'Everywhere I went friendly children would gather round me and I wondered why they were not at their lessons. I visited the local school and was shocked at the lack of teaching facilities and the small number of pupils in attendance.

'The teacher explained only a very few children could go to school because their parents could not afford the fees and the cost of the obligatory uniforms. From what he told me, I worked out the sum required to pay for a child to attend school for a year was equal to £10 sterling.

'The teacher asked me if I could help. I had never had any intention of starting a charity, it had never crossed my mind. But now I was there and saw the situation, I could not say "No".'

Roger went on to relate how on his return to Britain he started persuading family members and friends to sponsor a Mankoadze child so that he or she could attend school. Such was the response that soon the TEABAG charity came into being.

At the time Roger was talking to Tom, more than 300 children were being educated, a library of essential school books had been provided and funds had been raised for vital medical operations, all thanks to TEABAG.

'We watch out for medical emergencies when we can,' Roger continued. 'We have a project for the elderly and we try to encourage education for women.

'TEABAG is a small charity and it should stay that way because that is where the reward and pleasure is – knowing exactly what we are doing, knowing the people and the children personally and enjoying their progress. Some of the children have done very well.'

A typical classroom

He went on to emphasise that every penny TEABAG received was spent on the operation in Ghana. There was no media advertising, no leaflets requesting donations, no direct mailing – and no remuneration for work done in the UK. This was all voluntary. Money came from private donations and events such as sponsored runs, afternoon teas and summer barbecues. Supporters of the charity had learned about it entirely by word of mouth.

Roger ended his narrative by saying, 'I feel privileged to be taking part in this remote rural African community with a different history, culture and background... this has really become my life's work.'

Describing Tom's reaction to the TEABAG story, Roger later told the author, 'He told me he'd like to sponsor a child. Seeing him standing there with no arms I wondered how he would pay but a moment later his foot landed on the table with a £20 note between his toes.'

An aspect of Tom's character is his enthusiasm for beneficent organisations such as PHAB, CRYPT and Business in the Community. Now TEABAG became his new interest.

'To start with, Lucy and I sponsored a child, a little girl named Stella,' Tom says. 'Roger regularly sent us news of her progress. After a few months he told us that he wanted to take the charity one step further and get it registered properly, and to do this he needed trustees. I was invited to put my name forward. So that is what I did and I became a TEABAG trustee.'

A couple of years passed after Tom became involved with the TEABAG charity and one day Roger told him, 'You can't be a trustee and not know exactly what we are doing at Mankoadze.' And he suggested that Tom should go out to Ghana and see for himself. It was a suggestion that appealed to Tom.

So, in October 2007, Tom, carrying his visa and the obligatory yellow fever vaccination certificate, boarded an Accra-bound plane in company with

Stella, the girl sponsored by Tom and Lucy through the TEABAG project

Roger and several other TEABAG trustees. Being an inveterate traveller, he welcomed the opportunity of flying to a faraway land.

When he stepped out of the aircraft on to the tarmac of the Accra airport and felt the heat and unfamiliar atmosphere of Africa, a feeling of excitement replaced the tedium of the six-and-a-half hour flight – a feeling he was to experience again and again.

A hire car was waiting for the TEABAG party and soon Tom found himself surrounded by the colour, hubbub and jostle of an African city. People, either in jeans or brightly coloured robes, thronged the sidewalks which were lined with stalls of exotic-looking goods and shops, some of which had massive loudspeakers booming popular music to draw in customers. The noise was added to by taxis whose drivers continuously sounded their horns to advertise their availability as they edged through the congested streets.

Tom saw that when the traffic came to a halt, daring hawkers – men, women and children – raced among the vehicles holding up their wares which ranged from dried fish to toilet rolls, unfamiliar vegetables to chewing gum.

When the car broke free from the congestion and started along the coast road, Tom was told that the drive to Mankoadze would take an hour and a half. Before it had been built with Japanese aid, the journey took three and a half hours.

The artist in Tom was vividly reminded of Erich Stegmann's African paintings. No doubt he felt an urge to follow in the steps of the master and capture on canvas the hues of the palm-scattered landscape beneath the hot sky, with its clusters of small, brightly painted houses.

After a while, the car turned on to a rough clay road and bounced along in the direction of Mankoadze. The journey ended at a guesthouse close to the village, overlooking a beach of white sand on which graceful dugout fishing canoes were drawn up.

Early the next morning Tom set out to explore the place he had come so far to see. As he walked along the track leading from the guesthouse into the village, he met several local people and became aware of the natural friendliness that seems to permeate Ghana. He found it was the custom for a complete stranger to be given a broad smile, wished well and offered a welcoming hand. Tom's 'one regret' returned – he was unable to shake the proffered hands but mutual nods and grins made up for that.

Tom found Mankoadze to consist of one-storey dwellings, mostly with walls of mud or ancient concrete blocks, with roofs of rusting corrugated iron. These bordered narrow lanes along which amiable goats wandered. Here and there a woman would be crouching over her steaming cooking pot balanced on two blackened stones, with a fire of sticks burning between them.

Rumour had spread that a man without arms had arrived at the guesthouse and children flocked to see Tom. What impressed him was how well-mannered they were. For those who attended school, English was part of their education and it became a ritual for them to ask him 'What is your name?' The reply was 'Tom. What is your name?'

The child would give his or her name – often it had a Biblical connotation – and join the little crowd that was following Tom as though he was the Pied Piper.

When these introductions were completed one child asked, 'Mr Tom, why have you no arms?'

Tom explained that he had been born that way and anticipating further questions, said that he could use his feet just as they used their hands.

'Show us, Mr Tom, show us.'

'All right,' said Tom and kicked off his shoes. To amuse his young audience he produced a piece of paper and to their huge amusement drew funny figures on it with a pencil held between his toes. And when he did a lightning sketch of a little boy, children pointed to themselves and shouted, 'Me! Me!'

Next Tom performed a trick that went back to hours of practice in his boyhood days. With the toes of his left foot he produced a coin from his shoe and placed it on the top of his right foot. This demonstration of foot manipulation was greeted enthusiastically but the climax was yet to come.

'Watch!' ordered Tom and jerked his foot upwards. The coin spun high into the air and then as it began to fall he caught it on the back of his neck to cries of admiration.

Later in the day he was introduced to a number of the adult villagers including the venerable Nana George and the lady known as the Queen Mother. He noticed how easily his fellow trustees discussed with parents the progress of their wide-eyed children with whom they joked and addressed by name. In the following days he met the first group of children that TEABAG had supported and who had gained their JSS, the Ghanaian equivalent of the GCSE.

One member of the Trust had brought a very large suitcase full of trendy clothing which had been chosen in London for some of the girls.

Nana George, Queen Mother and Tom

No wonder the arrival of TEABAG members was always regarded as a time for jubilation.

Tom was also introduced to a boy named Ebenezer Otwe who had been born with legs so deformed that it was impossible for him to walk until TEABAG paid for him to have a series of operations. Now he was able to move about with the aid of crutches.

Late one afternoon Tom was walking through the village having had a talk with the Queen Mother when a voice called, 'Hello, Tom.'

'I recognised it as Ebenezer,' Tom recalls. 'For no reason I can remember, I said to him, "Hello Ebenezer, where do you live?" It was so automatic I don't think it was me saying it. It was like somebody else.'

'I show you,' was the reply. He got up on his crutches and Tom followed him out of the village and along a track until they reached a decrepit dwelling. It was little more than a roof of palm leaves supported on four poles above crumbling walls without glazed windows or basic amenities.

'It was loud and clear as if someone was speaking to me directly. It said, "This is why you are here."'

'Home,' said Ebenezer resting on his crutches. Shocked by the impoverished scene Tom could think of nothing to say. Then something happened that he believes was a mystical experience.

'I cannot explain it but at that moment I heard a voice in my head,' Tom says. 'It was loud and clear, as if someone was speaking to me directly. It said, "This is why you are here."'

The significance of these words was soon to become apparent.

One evening Tom and his fellow trustees were relaxing on the guesthouse verandah, watching the sun set over the sea while Roger Gillman entertained them with his guitar. A teacher from the local school which was attended by the TEABAG-sponsored children came and joined them.

In discussing his pupils he said, 'The problem is that when they have passed their primary school exams there is little chance of them furthering their education. While they can read, write and add up, they are unlikely to get work without going to college and learning some useful craft or trade. With such large numbers of young people in Ghana, there is great competition for jobs. Some of our children will most likely end up selling chewing gum on street corners.'

He went on to explain the reason only a few children were able to continue their education after primary school was that in Ghana the annual college fee was £200, while the average adult wage was less than £1 a day. Added to that the nearest college was quite a distance away, which meant more expense paying for accommodation.

The teacher's words set Tom thinking and he said to his fellow trustees, 'Why don't we build a college?'

Such a suggestion might have seemed preposterous; while it was one thing to pay for children to go to primary school, the prospect of setting up a college in a foreign country was daunting. But TEABAG trustees shared Tom's enthusiasm and it was decided to explore the possibilities of undertaking such a venture.

The first step was to find a suitable site.

According to Tom, Nana George was very keen on the idea and offered TEABAG a piece of land on which there was a ruinous carpenter's

The view from Kekes Beach Lodge

shack. It was ideally located as it was the first building to be seen when approaching the village.

'So the space was measured up and I said goodbye to my new friends and went back to my computer in the Selborne gallery,' Tom recalls. With his toes busy on the keyboard he set about designing the projected college, which apart from the usual classrooms, required facilities for vocational training. Work began soon after the plans were completed and Tom made several trips to Ghana to check on its progress.

Before long the walls were erected and the roof was up.

'It took about a year to complete, with me going back and forth,' Tom says. 'At one time we just painted the floor and the next time we had raised enough money to tile it.'

'Tom wanted it to be a vocational college, to teach marketable skills in the hope that the students would be able to

The ramshackle hut that was to form the basis of the new college

get good jobs with salaries,' Roger Gillman told the author. 'He is so keen and has so much energy that we went along with him.

'The building that we were given was a ramshackle old shed. The pillars were made from coconut trees and it was not a good structure at all. Tom designed the college building around this shell and we built it. Tom is a very good fundraiser and for a charity he is a tremendous

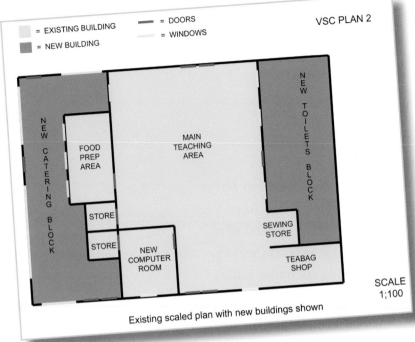

= EXISTING BUILDING
= NEW BUILDING
= DOORS
= WINDOWS

VSC PLAN 2

NEW CATERING BLOCK

FOOD PREP AREA

STORE

STORE

NEW COMPUTER ROOM

MAIN TEACHING AREA

NEW TOILETS BLOCK

SEWING STORE

TEABAG SHOP

SCALE 1;100

Existing scaled plan with new buildings shown

Above: Tom's plan for the new college and below: the completed building

asset. His energy can wear you out. He was on the go and concentrating on the college from the moment he woke up to the moment he dropped into bed. And he has raised money for it. We are very grateful for Tom's skills and the effort he has put into it.'

Tom wanted Lucy to visit Mankoadze to see the TEABAG project so in December 2008 Tom took her, Joe and Holly and his nephew to Ghana with a TEABAG trustee group.

'In the village we arranged a Christmas party for 300 children,' Tom says. 'We had gone shopping for supplies and the Queen Mother and her ladies cooked chicken and rice for everyone.

'We played party games and all were given food, ice lollies and bottles of Coke. My nephew dressed up in a Father Christmas costume and nearly died of the heat, while the kids shook hands with him and each received a present. It might have been the first present they had ever received in their lives.

'In the evening our party went back to the guesthouse, sat round the table and ate things like mince pies and Christmas pudding. It was a lovely day to remember.'

The TEABAG Christmas party has now become an annual event in Mankoadze.

✷✷✷

The college at Mankoadze is not the only building that Tom has designed on his computer. Recently he and Lucy decided to have a new house that would be tailored to their needs. Tom had learned of a company in Poland that specialised in making prefabricated houses to a client's plans. When the various components, including such necessities as plumbing, were completed at the factory they would be trucked to the client's prepared site and assembled.

This form of construction fascinated Tom who, with Lucy, decided their next house would be a prefabricated one made according to their special requirements. It would be built on a site by their existing house which meant that Tom would still be close to the Selborne gallery and Treloar College. His enthusiasm for the project must have reminded his parents of how he enjoyed drawing plans of buildings when he was a little boy.

The great advantage of Tom's design for the new house was that it would be built to make life as easy as possible for him. In particular the kitchen was planned so that he could work there without difficulty, a very important factor as Tom enjoys his cooking sessions. But his greatest satisfaction was designing a spacious, light-filled studio which would be exactly as he had always wanted.

Tom's printouts were sent to Poland, planning permission obtained, the site prepared and the bespoke house began to take shape.

****

While this book was being written the author visited Mankoadze in company with Tom and some TEABAG trustees. As the car carrying the party from the Accra airport came to a temporary standstill in the city congestion, street traders and mendicants scurried along the line of stationary vehicles.

'There's a man with only one arm,' someone said.

Tom, whose sense of humour is always close to the surface, exclaimed, 'I ought to go over and tell him how lucky he is!'

When the car neared its destination, it passed a large roadside sign which proclaimed 'Mankoadze Vocational Skills Centre'. Nearby stood a long white building which Tom eyed with affection and interest as though checking if some work on it had been completed.

Tom is often followed by a crowd of children as if he were the Pied Piper

A minute after the visitors arrived at Mankoadze a wave of children appeared and raced towards the car chorusing at the top of their voices, 'Mr Tom! Mr Tom!'

Their hero had returned.

As soon as he could, Tom went to the college which is spacious and airy, a comfort in the African climate. Adjoining the main hall was a large kitchen for girls taking the catering course, a room with sewing machines devoted to dressmaking and textile design, a workshop for boys and – Tom's pride – a special room where students sat at two rows of computers.

Sarah Garwood and Ann Vint with some of the TEABAG college's catering students

'There was an intake of 54 students in our first year and we started with four courses,' he said. 'IT was obvious because it is becoming a big subject in Africa. We now have twelve computers with satellite connections to the Internet and it enables the kids to do so much.

'Catering is important because if you can cook there are possibilities of working in hotels. There are courses in dressmaking and textile design for the girls, and practical training for boys hoping to get into construction work. We also run a course in business studies, but it is important that all students carry on their main subjects of English, maths and so forth as well as their vocational work.

'Last year we had four National Service people to help us. In Ghana you have to do National Service but if you have something you can offer, like teaching, you can do your service as a teacher in a school.'

Soon after his arrival Tom met Ebenezer. It was a happy reunion because although he was still dependent on his crutches, Ebenezer was doing well at school. He has been trained to operate the TEABAG video camera and records the major events of the village.

During the visit to Mankoadze, a wind gauge was set up on a nearby hill to record the average strength of the wind blowing in from the Atlantic. This was to check if it would be suitable to drive a wind turbine to provide electricity for the college and the village.

Ghana is in a position to take advantage of modern technology. For example, when Roger Gillman first visited the village, he found that to make a telephone call involved a round trip to Winneba, a town ten miles away, where there was a shack with a single telephone. Now TEABAG college computers can connect with the Internet and it is possible to use a mobile phone in an area where telephone lines have never existed.

A course at the TEABAG college lasts for three years. The students start work at 7.15 in the morning and carry on until 2 o'clock in the afternoon, which is the end of their official day. However, most return of their own accord to do their homework in the evening.

Visitors to Mankoadze, such as the author, come away deeply impressed by the college and the speed with which it was built and began functioning. Equally they are heartened by the students' extraordinary enthusiasm for the vital courses and stimulation they provide.

Ebenezer has been trained to be TEABAG's camera-operator

Tom has always had the support of a strong and loving family, not least his parents Jack and Margaret

Chapter 12

Fifty years have passed since the devastating effects of the 'wonder drug' thalidomide became apparent, and Tom is celebrating his 50th birthday. He laughs as he says he has beaten the medical prognosis by a decade.

Looking back on his life Tom says, 'If a little fairy came along and sprinkled moon dust on me and said, "You can be born again with arms", I don't think I would want it.'

This may seem to be a strange thing for a disabled person to say but Tom does not regard himself as disabled.

'I feel I've never had a disability in my life,' he says. 'People may think that you must struggle not having arms but when you've grown up with it, you know your abilities. Just because you use your feet to do things in a different way doesn't make you disabled.'

But Tom admits that sometimes he still finds it can be a little embarrassing to go out in public.

'I don't feel uneasy,' he explains. 'I just find it easier not to have to explain myself. I am happy to go to a swimming pool, put on my swimming trunks and dive in. But kids say things like "Look Mum, that man over there hasn't any arms.' What affects me is the embarrassment they feel over the fact that I am without arms.'

Tom is adamant that he has been extraordinarily lucky.

'I believe in luck, and the odd thing is that the harder I work the luckier I get.'

'I was lucky that I was born into a strong and loving family,' he says. 'They gave me all the encouragement I needed but were wise enough not to do too much for me so that I learned to look after myself. Growing up with an older brother and three sisters, I don't think I had a chance to feel sorry for myself.

'All the positive opportunities I have had come from the fact that I was born without arms.'

There can be no doubt that in combating his handicap, Tom gained the determination to make the best of his life.

'I should like to acknowledge what an understanding wife I have,' Tom says. 'I am so lucky with Lucy. Very few wives would allow their husbands just to get up and go off to foreign parts as I do with my visits to Ghana. Because she has been out there she knows what I am on about when I come back talking about Nana George and the Queen Mother, Ebenezer and the Mankoadze gossip. And she has been so helpful at exhibitions and at the gallery.

"You can give children money, computers and other possessions but the best thing you can give them is your time."

'When my son Joe was 18 months old, we went to see my grandmother who was in a nursing home. I think she was nearly 100 years old and it was the last time we saw her. After an hour we got up to go and she said to me, "There is one piece of advice I want to give you."

'I've always remembered what she told me.

'"You can give children money, computers and other possessions but the best thing you can give them is your time."'

Her words became a credo with Lucy and Tom, and he says, 'I think Joe and Holly have turned out well, even though I say it myself. I am just so proud of them. That comes through hard work at being a fantastic parent and that's down to Lucy.'

Tom has led a remarkably full life, with no sign of slowing down yet. His many varied interests have given him ample opportunity to make use of his organising abilities, ranging from early youth club work to the setting up of the Selborne gallery. In recent years he has been deeply concerned with the TEABAG charity and the establishment of the Mankoadze College, yet his first love remains the MFPA.

'Even though I am deeply involved with TEABAG, the MFPA is my life,' Tom declares. 'I am so lucky and I put it all down to the fact I am a member of the Association. Through it I became a professional artist and I enjoy other activities such as the mobile gallery, organising exhibitions and giving talks on our work. I am so honoured to be part of such a wonderful organisation.'

To celebrate the MFPA's 50th anniversary, Tom organised an exhibition, which was held at the Royal College of Art in October 2006. Here David Shepherd, the renowned wildlife artist, unveils a painting made up of 20 panels, each painted by a different UK MFPA artist. The subject is a work entitled 'Floating Market in Bangkok' by the Association's founder Erich Stegmann

✳✳✳✳

In a number of ways Tom emulates Erich Stegmann who, as well as being a highly successful artist, created the MFPA. He travelled the world on its behalf and was always mindful of those that he could help.

'I believe we are born for a reason,' Tom says. 'I believe my purpose is to be a living example of how difficulties can be overcome. Someone with a difficulty might say, "If Tom can do it without arms, I can do it with hands."

'When my father had a stroke and found it difficult to bend down and put his socks on he said to my mother, "If Tom can do it I can do it." And he did. So if that is an attitude I can give people, that's what I am here for.'

This book began with a quotation and now ends with another applicable to Tom, who believes that he is so lucky. A well-known author once said, 'I believe in luck, and the odd thing is that the harder I work the luckier I get.'

Tom with his wife Lucy and children Holly and Joe

Tom's design to commemorate the AMFPA's 50th anniversary

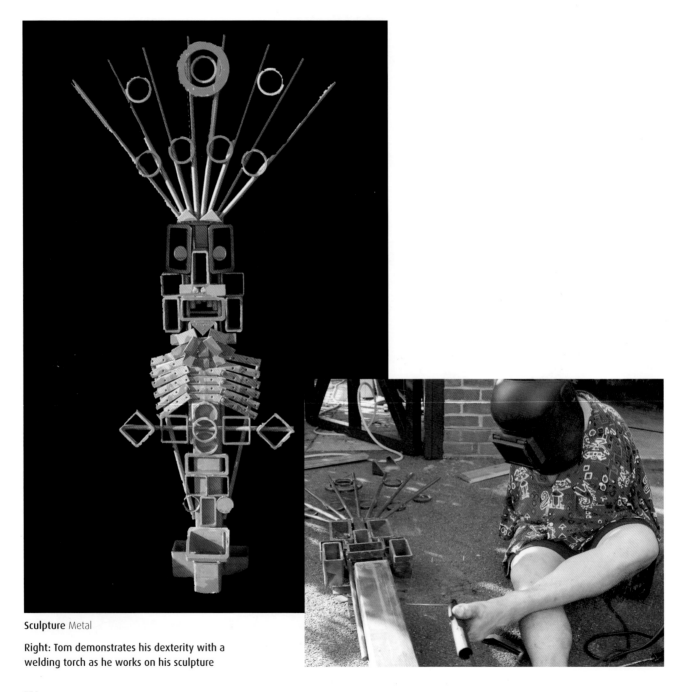

Sculpture Metal

Right: Tom demonstrates his dexterity with a welding torch as he works on his sculpture

Useful links

To find out more about Tom and his passions and interests, please take a look at the following websites:

www.vdmfk.com	Association of Mouth and Foot Painting Artists worldwide website
www.mfpa.co.uk	Mouth and Foot Painting Artists UK website
www.teabagcharity.org.uk	The project in Ghana
www.tomyendell.co.uk	Tom's own website

About the author

Before becoming a full-time author Marc Alexander was a schoolteacher who had majored in art, a Fleet Street journalist and a magazine editor. During his boyhood in New Zealand, he experienced a period of disability due to a spinal ailment, which required a year in traction with little movement. He says that this has helped him to fully appreciate the amazing endeavour of mouth and foot painting artists. He has had over 60 books published, both fiction and non-fiction. He found those he has written about members of the MFPA have been the most fascinating to work on. Much of his writing is done at his cottage in Cumbria and his favourite form of relaxation has been his canal cruiser *Blue Flame*.